LIFE TOGETHER *IN* CHRIST

EXPERIENCING TRANSFORMATION
IN COMMUNITY

RUTH HALEY BARTON

IVP Books

An imprint of InterVarsity Press
Downers Grove, Illinois

InterVarsity Press
P.O. Box 1400, Downers Grove, IL 60515-1426
ivpress.com
email@ivpress.com

InterVarsity Press® is the book-publishing division of InterVarsity Christian Fellowship/USA®, a movement of
students and faculty active on campus at hundreds of universities, colleges and schools of nursing in the United
States of America, and a member movement of the International Fellowship of Evangelical Students. For
information about local and regional activities, visit intervarsity.org.

Scripture quotations, unless otherwise noted, are from the New Revised Standard Version of the Bible,
copyright 1989 by the Division of Christian Education of the National Council of the Churches of Christ in
the USA. Used by permission. All rights reserved.

While any stories in this book are true, some names and identifying information may have been changed to
protect the privacy of individuals.

Cover design: Cindy Kiple
Interior design: Beth McGill
Images: The Road to Emmaus by Daniel Bonnell

ISBN 978-0-8308-3586-7 (hardcover)
ISBN 978-0-8308-9638-7 (digital)

Printed in the United States of America ∞

As a member of the Green Press Initiative, InterVarsity Press is committed to protecting
the environment and to the responsible use of natural resources. To learn more, visit
greenpressinitiative.org.

Library of Congress Cataloging-in-Publication Data

Barton, R. Ruth, 1960-
    Life together in Christ / Ruth Haley Barton.
        pages cm
    Includes bibliographical references.
    ISBN 978-0-8308-3586-7 (hardcover : alk. paper)
    1. Spiritual formation. 2. Communities—Religious
aspects—Christianity. I. Title.
    BV4511.B27 2014
    248.4—dc23

                                                    2014033346

P   21   20   19   18   17   16   15   14   13   12   11   10   9   8   7   6   5   4   3   2

Y   32   31   30   29   28   27   26   25   24   23   22   21   20   19   18   17   16   15

For the communities of the Transforming Center

with deepest gratitude for our

life together in Christ

And for my family—

the richest and most life-transforming

community of all

CONTENTS

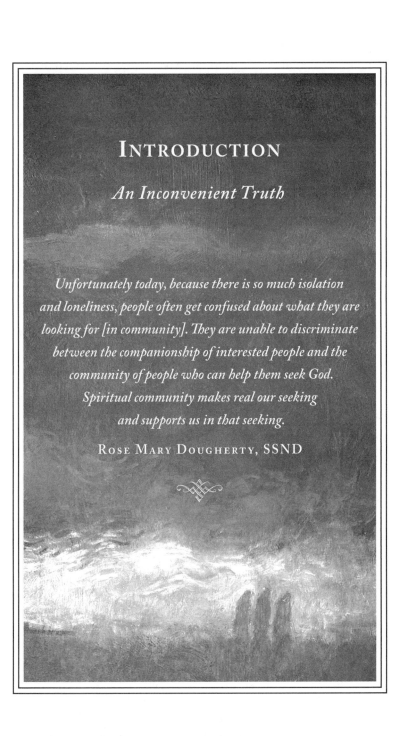

INTRODUCTION

An Inconvenient Truth

*Unfortunately today, because there is so much isolation
and loneliness, people often get confused about what they are
looking for [in community]. They are unable to discriminate
between the companionship of interested people and the
community of people who can help them seek God.
Spiritual community makes real our seeking
and supports us in that seeking.*

ROSE MARY DOUGHERTY, SSND

"Community is the most 'overpromised and underdelivered' aspect of the church today," a friend who has been involved with many different kinds of churches commented many years ago. This haunting observation is one I have never been able to forget. I couldn't figure out whether to laugh or cry, so I think I did both.

The more I have reflected on his statement, the more I have had to acknowledge the truth in it. Having been in and around the church all my life—first as a pastor's kid, then as a congregant, and then as a leader—I, too, have grown skeptical. When I hear people speak in glowing terms about their vision for community, I have my doubts. When they tell me about painful things that have happened to them in community, I am never surprised. How many of us have joined a church or some other kind of spiritually minded group in hopes of experiencing real care, connection and belonging, only to be disappointed? How often have we sat through inspiring sermons about what is possible when Christians gather together in mutually edifying relationships, only to recognize how cynical we have become after many failed attempts? Whether it's an overtly religious group or not, there is something about human beings trying to get together and function together over the long haul that is just plain difficult.

There is another overpromised, underdelivered aspect of the church today that is equally disillusioning, and that is the promise of spiritual transformation. One of the great mysteries of my growing-up years as a pastor's kid was watching the people in our church and noticing that some of them were just not changing. Many of them remained selfish, stuck in their ways (not to mention stuck in bad marriages and dysfunctional families) and spiritually lifeless—conditions that only seemed to worsen over time. Then, as I became a grown-up in the church, I sometimes noticed the same thing about myself! Even though I participated fully in the life of the community and served there faithfully, I too had to acknowledge that I was not changing. Although I could sometimes get better at controlling negative behavior and hiding my bad attitudes, I was not being transformed at the deepest levels of my being. I made the disheartening discovery that it is possible to hang around other Christians a lot, meet regularly for worship, study our Bibles, join a church and even call ourselves a community but *not change at all* in ways that count. Talk about an inconvenient truth!

THE PROMISE OF SPIRITUAL TRANSFORMATION

A recent Barna survey found that a majority of self-identified Christians today (52 percent) believe that there is much more to the Christian life than they have experienced, and 46 percent say their life has not changed at all as a result of going to church. What about you? Are you one of them? Do you ever let yourself imagine what it might be like to be part of a transforming community—rather than a deforming community—one in which people regularly and routinely experience real life change rather than staying stuck in their ways? Or in some deep, inarticulate place have you decided it's too much to hope for?

But no matter how cynical we have become, the promise that we—sin-scarred human beings that we are—can become like Christ is one of the great promises of the gospel (e.g., Galatians 4:19). Salvation is not merely about knowing where we are going when we die; it is also about the possibility of kingdom living here and now. It is about being fundamentally changed in the depths of our being so that the will of God can be done *in our lives* on earth as it is in heaven.

Spiritual transformation is the process by which Christ is formed in us—for the glory of God, for the abundance of our own lives and for the sake of others; it results in an increasing capacity to discern and do the will of God. Spiritual transformation in the lives of redeemed people is a testimony to the power of the gospel; indeed, it is an act of worship in which our very lives testify or ascribe worth to the One who made us, who calls us by name and redeems us for his purposes. For all these reasons and more, *spiritual transformation is central to the message of the gospel and therefore central to the mission of the church.*

As fundamental and essential as it is, spiritual transformation is also something of a paradox. It is *natural* for Christ-followers to grow and change, just as it is natural for human beings to grow from infancy to childhood to adolescence to adulthood. The seed of the Christ-life ("everything we need for life and godliness") is planted within us at salvation, and if the conditions are right, that seed will grow and flourish. At the same time, the process of transformation is also *supernatural* in that it is something only God can accomplish in our lives through the work of the Holy Spirit. It is one of the great mysteries of our faith that takes place in and through the Trinity, as God transforms us into the image of Christ through the real presence of the Holy Spirit. We can find ways to be open to this miraculous work of God, but we cannot control it or make it happen—in ourselves or anyone else. The wind of the Spirit blows where it wills.

And yet even though we cannot transform ourselves, there *is* something we *can* do: we can create the conditions in which spiritual transformation takes place. That is where spiritual disciplines come in. Spiritual disciplines are concrete activities we can engage in for the purpose of making ourselves available to God for the work only God can do. Some of those disciplines take place as we are alone with God in solitude. Others take place in community with other Christ-followers—which is the topic of this book. And still others take place in the world beyond the community as we share our faith, serve the poor, show compassion, work for justice and seek reconciliation. These disciplines or practices are what Paul was referring to when he appealed to the Christians in Rome to "present your bodies as a living sacrifice, holy and acceptable to God, which is your spiritual worship" (Romans 12:1). He was simply talking about finding ways to surrender to God in every aspect of life—not just in theory but in reality.

Participating intentionally and meaningfully in transforming community is one of those ways.

THE POWER OF COMMUNITY

Spiritual transformation takes place *incrementally over time with others in the context of disciplines and practices that open us to God.* In general, while we are still on this earth, our transformation will happen by degrees (2 Corinthians 3:18), and we need each other in order to grow (1 Corinthians 12).

Paul's teachings on spiritual growth and transformation in Romans 12 and other epistles are always given in the context of community—the body of Christ with its many members. He waxes eloquent about the fact that we are given to one another for mutual edification, to spur one another on to love and good deeds. Our spiritual gifts are not given to us for our own benefit; they are given to the body of Christ so that together we can be all we are meant to be. In community, others become "agents of God's troubling grace" for our further growth and transformation, and we become the same for them; as each part functions properly, it "promotes the body's growth in building itself up in love" (Ephesians 4: 15-16).[1] As Robert Mulholland writes, "We can no more be conformed to the image of Christ outside corporate spirituality than a coal can continue to burn outside of the fire."[2]

In this way we begin to see that transformation and community are integrally related. It is the lack of spiritual transformation within individuals and systems that causes communities to falter and sometimes implode or explode. And it is the lack of community—a privatized approach to transformation that fails to see other people as necessary instruments of God's grace—that limits the work of transformation in our lives. If we can bring these two dynamics together in *transforming community*, a spontaneous combustion will begin to take place. But given what we have so often witnessed in Christian communities, how does the *possibility* of transformation in community become the *reality* in our settings?

FINDING OUR WAY

Transforming community begins to emerge as we establish *shared understanding* about what spiritual transformation is, develop *shared language* for talking about and encouraging one another in the process, and embrace a *shared commitment* to arranging our lives for spiritual transformation. This involves so much more than adding a program or offering an elective class, and it doesn't happen by accident. In a transforming community, the value and the priority of spiritual transformation is taught, discussed and lived out in large groups and in small groups, in families and among friends, in formal Christian education settings and informal conversations. It becomes central to the life of the community, just as eating and breathing are essential to life in a physical body. Structured opportunities and appropriate resources are offered, while at the same time there is great reverence and respect for the spontaneous bubbling up of the Spirit's work in people's lives.

Becoming a transforming community involves having real guidance in the attitudes, practices and behaviors that open us to the transforming presence of Christ in our midst. And that's where a book like this comes in. *Life Together in Christ* is an interactive guide for small groups of people who are ready to get personal and practical about experiencing transformation together. Hopefully there are pastors and leaders in the community who are preaching and casting vision for transforming community—assuring us that such things are possible; however, it is also understood that certain kinds of growth, attention and support can only take place in smaller settings where relationships are being cultivated for this purpose— small groups that meet in homes, Christian education settings, boards and ministry teams, mission groups and the like. Rather than being required to have such experiences, people are drawn in or invited into these opportunities on the basis of shared desire.

This book is designed to function on two levels at once—both personal and communal. You will notice that there are gray boxes throughout each chapter; their content is designed to spark individuals' personal reflection. Group members may want to start a notebook or a journal for recording these thoughts, prayers and reflections. Then at the end of each chapter there is a section titled "On the Road Together" that is designed for group process and interactions. These will include some combination of discussion questions, spiritual exercises, practices and prayers that the group will engage in together when members gather. This interactive process will work best if individuals are able carve out time to read and reflect on the content of each chapter before the group meeting so they will be prepared to engage fully, contributing thoughtfully and substantively to the group process.

THE EMMAUS ROAD AS A MODEL

The New Testament account of two disciples who were finding their way home from Jerusalem to Emmaus following the most traumatic weekend of their lives is a compelling example of how we can experience transforming community in the most unexpected places. *Life Together in Christ* will unpack this story, found in Luke 24, piece by piece, drawing attention to many of the community practices that enable us to open to Christ together—choosing to walk together; welcoming the stranger; practicing hospitality; paying attention to our deepest hopes and desires; experiencing prayer, worship and teaching as communal disciplines; breaking bread together; practicing discernment; and bearing witness. Be assured that we will do more than just think about the dynamic possibilities contained within these practices; we will actually experience them for ourselves.

Along the way, we will discover that our spiritual transformation is not for ourselves alone. It is both an end in itself—because human beings who are becoming like Christ bring glory to God—*and* a means to other ends having to do with sharing our faith and engaging the larger human community in Jesus' name. Communities that gather in Christ's name to be Christ's presence in the world will order their lives in such a way that they actually can *experience* the abundant life Jesus promises and thus bear witness in the world around them. Anything less just will not do.

> Ultimately, the presence that transforms is not ours, nor is it that of the other person we encounter. The transformational presence is that of the One who is with us in the encounter.
>
> David Benner

As we are changed into more loving, surrendered Christ-followers, we *become* the presence of Christ in the world that God loves and sent his only Son to save. We are able to join others on whatever hard road they are traveling and discern loving, God-guided response to their need. We learn that, indeed, all true Christian spiritual formation is for the glory of God, for the abundance of our own lives and for the sake of others, or it is not *Christian* formation. With the apostle Paul we affirm, "It is [Christ] whom we proclaim, . . . teaching everyone in all wisdom, so that we may present everyone mature [fully formed] in Christ. For this I toil and struggle with all the energy that he powerfully inspires within me" (Colossians 1:28-29).

CHOOSING TO WALK THE ROAD TOGETHER

Before choosing to get on the road together, your group will do well to discuss some of the ideas presented in this introduction and consider whether embarking on an intentional journey of transformation in community is something you want to explore. To start, reflect together on the opening illustrations and comments on "the most overpromised, underdelivered" aspects of the church today. Do you agree? Disagree? What have your past experiences of community and spiritual transformation been? How have these experiences affected you?

Do you ever let yourself imagine what it might be like to be part of a transforming community? What would you give to experience that, or does it even matter to you right now? Is there any way in which you have given up?

How do you respond to the statement that "spiritual transformation is central to the message of the gospel and therefore central to the mission of the church"? Do you agree? Disagree? How does this motivate you (or not) to participate in a transforming community?

I have provided many scriptural references to offer a basic biblical and theological perspective on transformation, its centrality to the gospel, the role of the Trinity and in particular the Holy Spirit, the natural and supernatural aspects of it, the role of spiritual disciplines, the necessity of community, and its being for the sake of others. Take time to actually read the Scriptures cited here; if you would like a more complete listing of Scripture passages on spiritual transformation, see appendix A. How do you respond to these scriptural truths? Which ones inspire you? Which create more questions? What are you most interested in exploring further, alone or as a group?

What is your level of enthusiasm for and commitment to experiencing the practices related to experiencing transformation in community?

Be sure to discuss these questions together before going on.

BETWEEN THE NOW AND THE NOT YET

Choosing to Walk Together

Now on that same day two of them were going to a village called Emmaus, about seven miles from Jerusalem, and talking with each other about all these things that had happened . . .

LUKE 24:13-14

What do you think of when you think of community? I'm serious. I want you to stop and think about what comes to your mind when you hear or see the word *community*. Do you see visions of backyard barbecues with adults talking and laughing easefully while children play in the yard? Earnest Christians sitting in well-appointed living rooms with coffee poured and Bibles open, searching the Scriptures? Do you see people caring for one another in times of crisis—meals brought when someone is sick, a pastor rushing to the bedside of a dying church member, childcare and other kinds of support offered when needed?

How about accountability groups where people confess their struggles with sin and check in with one another regularly about how it's going? Or support groups gathering on the basis of affinity around issues like gender, marital status, life stage, various addictions or even a desire to lose weight? Maybe a community group of neighbors rallying together to lobby and raise money for improvements in their neighborhood or precinct?

Another possibility is that when you think of community you are flooded with painful memories—a church split you got caught up in, a small group that fell apart because of a disagreement or an unresolved conflict, a denomination that couldn't resolve theological differences and splintered, a pastor who preached convincingly about community but then failed to live it out with his or her own community, a factious elder group or ministry board that stood publicly for Christian ideals but failed to practice them privately. Perhaps you have had a painful falling out with a close neighbor about a matter of shared concern, and even though you attempted to work things out, you are still in deep disagreement. Just living on the same street is now awkward and difficult—you find yourselves ducking quickly into your respective homes so as to avoid contact.

If any of these have been your experience, you may have quietly settled into a state of cynicism, going through the motions of being friendly in community contexts but knowing in the deep places of your heart that you have given up.

For Personal Reflection

What comes to your mind when you think of the word *community*? What experiences have shaped you?

WHEN THE WISH DREAM DIES

The scenarios described above conjure up either pleasant or disturbing images of what can happen—the good, the bad and the ugly—when human beings come together on the basis of a shared cause or some kind of natural affinity. But clearly that's not enough. While all of the experiences highlighted in the first two paragraphs can be wonderful and important aspects of community life, none of them capture *what community really is.*

It seems that one of the main reasons we are confused about community is that *we make it primarily about us*—our experiences and feelings, our natural affinities, our life situation, what we think we want or need, or some vision of what we're going to accomplish together. We labor under the mistaken idea that we can create community through something we bring to the table—casting a compelling vision, developing the right curriculum or plan, choosing the latest, greatest Bible study guide, training and supporting small group leaders just so, coming up with good icebreaker questions, creating a "safe" environment—and then we are disappointed when things fall apart or relationships fail to satisfy.

Ironically, such experiences of disappointment seem to be necessary in order for us to learn what the essence of life together in Christ really is. In fact, German pastor and theologian Dietrich Bonhoeffer states boldly that the sooner our "wish dream" about what community should be is shattered, the better it is for everyone.

> Innumerable times a whole Christian community has been broken down because it had sprung from a wish dream . . . but God's grace speedily shatters such dreams. Just as surely as God desires to lead us to a knowledge of genuine Christian fellowship, so surely must we be overwhelmed by a great disillusionment with others, with Christians in general, and, if we are fortunate, with ourselves.[1]

I have to admit that my first impulse on reading this particular passage was a strong desire to throw the book against the wall. (Clearly, I was still a bit too attached to my wish dream.) But as I settled down, ruminated over it a bit more and endured a few more death blows to my own wish dreams, Bonhoeffer's statements began to make sense. *Christian community is not and never can be about us.* When our dreams and convictions about what we think community should be are dashed against the jagged reef of human limitations and failure to live up to one another's needs and expectations, then and only then are we ready to accept the fact that Christian community is not about us at all. It is about the transforming presence of Christ—all *he will do* in and through and for each of us.

In the end, the death of our wish dream is really an occasion for great hope. As Bonhoeffer goes on to say, "Thus the very hour of disillusionment with my brother [or sister] becomes incomparably salutary, because it so thoroughly teaches me that neither of us can live by our own words and deeds, but only by that one Word and Deed which really binds us together. . . . When the morning mists of dreams vanish, then dawns the bright day of Christian fellowship."[2]

This is exactly where we find the two disciples on the road to Emmaus. Their "wish dream" about what life together with Christ was going to be like had vanished—violently ripped from them—and now a new day was dawning on a future they could not yet comprehend.

BETWEEN THE NOW AND THE NOT YET

The biblical account of this story begins with two dazed and distraught disciples traveling along the road from Jerusalem to Emmaus. It was Sunday, the third day of the most traumatic weekend of their lives, and they were on a roller coaster of emotion. On Friday these disciples along with many others had witnessed the painful, humiliating and violent death of their beloved leader, teacher and friend. That night and through the day on Saturday they sat with each other in utter despair. And now, on this day, a glimmer of hope had been introduced into the situation.

Some of the women in their group had visited the tomb in which their leader had been buried and found it empty. There was talk of resurrection, but it was too soon to tell whether it was a miracle or just a hoax of some sort. They had hung around in waiting mode as long as they could, and now it was time to get back to real life. Their dream of what the kingdom of God would look like as it had emerged from their little community, the hopes and dreams on which they had oriented the last three years of their lives, the vision that had caused them to give up fishing and tax collecting and the like in order to commit themselves to following Jesus—it was all gone. Each one who had been part of the community of Jesus now had to come to terms with life on the other side of the death of their wish dream. They had to figure out what to live for now that the vision that had brought order and purpose to their lives was no more.

Not knowing what else to do, Cleopas and an unnamed disciple were wandering home, trying to make sense of it all. They were suspended somewhere between loss and possible gain, grief and possible joy, profound human suffering and perhaps some kind of redemption, dashed hopes and maybe daring to hope again. They were wrung out—emotionally, spiritually and physically. They had been powerless to prevent the events of the last days, and they were powerless now to do anything to change their situation. *The road from Jerusalem to Emmaus was the road between the now and the not yet.*

Although they were probably not aware of it, these disciples were in what Richard Rohr calls "liminal space"—a particular spiritual position where human beings hate to be, but where the biblical God is always leading them. The Latin root *limen* literally means "threshold," referring to that needed transition when we are moving from one place or one state of being to another.[3] Liminal space usually induces some sort of inner crisis: you have left the tried and true (or it has left you), and you have not yet been able to replace it with anything else.

This is Abraham leaving his home country and his father's house for a land he did not yet know.

It is Joseph in the pit.

It is the Israelites wandering in the wilderness between Egypt and the Promised Land.

It is Jonah in the belly of the fish.

It is Mary weeping at Jesus' tomb.

It is the disciples huddled in the upper room.

It is Cleopas and the unnamed disciple on the Emmaus Road betwixt and between the life they had known and whatever was supposed to come next.

This was a time for intimate emotions and dangerous questions. Maybe something new and wonderful was in the works, but who knew? And just when they had gotten about the business of trying to adjust to their new normal, they were unnerved by the unexpected, pushed off center by intimations of the unimaginable.

Thank God they had each other!

FINDING OURSELVES ON THE ROAD

I am intrigued by the fact that the second disciple on the Emmaus Road is not named. Even though it's fun to speculate (some think the unnamed disciple was Cleopas's wife; others think it was Luke, who is attempting not to draw attention to himself), I prefer to leave it alone. The fact that we don't know who the second disciple was means it is easier for us to find ourselves on this familiar road. For you see, all of us are on our own Emmaus Road—somewhere between the now and the not yet—in some area of our lives.

The disrupting event could be something as traumatic as the loss of a job, the breakup of a marriage or some other close relationship, the death of a loved one, a betrayal of some sort where something has been taken from us forcibly and the new has not yet come. Or it could be something a little more subtle—like a sense that it is time to let go of one thing in order to be open to something new, a negative pattern we know is in need of further transformation, an awareness of a stuck place in our spiritual life where we don't know how to get unstuck. There is a sense that we, too, are waiting for something that has not yet been fully revealed.

While it may feel that whatever precipitated our Emmaus Road experience is beyond our control, we do have control over one thing: whether we will walk the road alone or choose to walk it with others. I don't know about you, but when I am in the throes of loss and disillusionment, profound emotions and dangerous questions, I usually want to keep to myself. Some things feel entirely too personal to share with others, and at such moments I am convinced that no one could possibly understand what I'm going through. The idea of trying to put the unspeakable into words feels completely exhausting, and the thought of subjecting my soul to inane questions and trite answers during such tender times is almost too much to bear.

The disciples' choice to walk together and talk about all the things that had happened to them was, in some ways, fairly radical. They could have decided that what they had been through was so personal, so traumatic and so confounding that they didn't want to talk about it until they had gotten a handle on it. Or they could have chosen to walk together but avoided talking about what was really going on, chatting away about anything else but *that*. But no. While the experiences of the weekend were still fresh and raw, unvarnished and unresolved, they chose to walk together and talk with each other about *all these things that had happened*.

The reason this was such a crucial choice was that there is something about the willingness to walk together and speak honestly about the fundamental issues of our lives that causes Jesus himself to come near.

The disciples on the Emmaus Road weren't praying in any formal way. They were not having a Bible study or worshiping in the synagogue. They were not having a formal quiet time. They were discussing the stuff of their lives—all the things that had happened that were having such an impact on them spiritually and in every other way—and something about the nature and quality of their conversation opened up space for Jesus to draw near. And the encounter that took place among them was completely reorienting and life changing.

That is the essence of Christian community. Before Jesus draws near, a group of people journeying together is merely a human community. Once Jesus joins us on the road, it becomes a Christian community. As we discover ways to open to Jesus' transforming presence on the road between the now and the not yet, it becomes a transforming community.

> ### *For Personal Reflection*
> In what area of your life do you experience *yourself* as being on the road between "the now and the not yet"?

TRANSFORMED IN CHRIST'S PRESENCE—OR NOT

It is interesting to reflect on the initial formation of Jesus' community and notice that Christian community begins with Jesus and his invitation *to be with him*. After a night of prayerful discernment, Jesus "called to him those whom he wanted." He called them first to be with him *and then* to be sent out into the world to accomplish his purposes—in that order (Mark 3:13-14). These called ones became Christ's community not because they were drawn to each other or were seeking some sort of extraordinary social experience; they were called first and foremost *to be with Jesus*, and by virtue of their relationship with Jesus they came into relationship with each other. Even as they journeyed together and relationships among them began to form, the focus was not so much on their direct relationships with each other as it was on continuing to be in a life-transforming relationship with Jesus. This relationship, in turn, impacted the nature and quality of their relationships with each other. Later in Mark 3 Jesus further clarifies the nature and the outcome of his true community when he says, "Here are my mother and my brothers! Whoever does the will of God is my brother and sister and mother" (vv. 34-35).

This may seem like a subtle distinction, but it is essential to clarify it in a culture where the idea of community has taken on so many meanings—most of which are focused on the human beings, human needs and human dynamics involved. When our clarity about the central focus of community gets muddled, it can devolve to the point where Jesus becomes almost secondary! Conversely, when individuals in groups make it their priority to recognize and respond to the transforming presence of Christ in their midst, they stand a lot better chance of maintaining transforming relationships in community.

Thus we are drawn to go one step further in our understanding of Christian community to cultivate *transforming* communities— *men and women gathered around the presence of Christ for the purpose of being transformed in Christ's presence so they can discern and do the will of God.* This involves clarifying and committing ourselves to concrete ways in which we will open to Christ's transforming presence together.

You might think that being transformed in Christ's presence is to be assumed, but I assure you it is not. The biblical record shows that *it is possible to hang around Jesus a lot and still not change.* If you don't believe me, consider Judas Iscariot, who was one of Jesus' twelve closest disciples and yet betrayed him in the end. All that hanging out did not appear to change him in any sort of fundamental way! *It is possible to walk with Jesus very closely and miss the whole point of Jesus' life.* Witness Peter's complete lack of understanding and actual resistance to God's will in Jesus' life—to the extent that Jesus finally had to say, "Get behind me, Satan!" *It is possible to love Jesus a lot and still succumb to fear rather than faith.* Consider the way in which Peter and many of the other disciples betrayed Jesus on the night of his death. It was like everything they had learned and experienced with Jesus went flying out the window under duress!

What was *that* about?

CHRIST FORMED IN US

Part of what that's about is that many of us don't understand what spiritual transformation is—really. We might think spiritual transformation has to do with mere behavioral tweaks—being able to control our anger or drinking a bit better or masking our selfishness and ego-drivenness a little more effectively. We might think the process of spiritual transformation is a natural byproduct of showing up at church services, giving our tithe and studying our Bible. Or we might associate it with warm, fuzzy retreat experiences or contemplative spiritual disciplines that appeal to a certain personality type. This is most assuredly not the case.

Spiritual transformation is the process by which Christ is formed in us—for the glory of God, for the abundance of our own lives and for the sake of others. It is central to the gospel and therefore central to the mission of the church and central to our lives as those who gather in Christ's name. When Paul wrote to the new communities of Christians springing up in places like Rome and Corinth and Galatia, he used two metaphors to help them understand the amazing possibility that the person and character of Christ could be formed in them. One was the metaphor of an embryo being formed in its mother's womb, and the other was the caterpillar entering into the cocoon and eventually emerging as an entirely different kind of creature with brand-new capacities. Both metaphors contain a bit of paradox: that spiritual transformation is a natural process for those in whom the seed of the Christ-life has been planted, but it is also supernatural in that it is a miracle—a God-thing—each and every time it happens.

To the church in Rome Paul wrote, "Do not be conformed to this world, but be transformed by the renewing of your minds" (Romans 12:2). Too often this leads us to conclude that spiritual transformation is primarily an intellectual process, so we study really hard and try to gain all the right information. This reductionist approach to formation is unfortunate because the Greek word *nous* (translated "mind") includes intellectual or cognitive knowing but goes far beyond it. This word denotes the seat of reflective consciousness—the thought patterns from which our behaviors originate. The mind encompasses both how we perceive and understand the world and the patterns of feeling, judging and determining that shape our actions and responses in the world. It is not only our beliefs and thought patterns but also the attitudes and behaviors that emerge from them that need to be transformed.

The mind functions in large part to protect the self, to figure things out on its own terms according to the relationships and experiences that have shaped it over time. The mind works hard to control and manage reality and has its own plans for remedying the human situation outside of Christ and abandonment to his divine will. Thomas Keating, in his work on the true self and the false, describes these plans as "emotional programs for happiness" based on childhood instinctual needs and all the ways we compensate for these unfulfilled needs. He identifies these basic, primal impulses as the following needs:

- safety/security/survival
- affection/esteem/approval
- power and control

All of these are legitimate human needs. The sin problem has to do with the fact that we have all developed unconscious ways of meeting these needs for ourselves on our own terms—to a greater or lesser extent—apart from God. Thus any approach to transformation that seeks to bring about real change must go beyond merely grasping information at the cognitive level to gaining full, experiential knowledge of God. Such knowledge changes our deepest inner orientations and trust structures, our false-self patterns, and any other obstacles and attachments that prevent us from fully surrendering to God.[4]

True transformation involves learning about the nature of the Christian life and the path to true change, yes, but this level of learning is only the beginning. We also need guidance for engaging in the behaviors, relationships, practices and experiences that open us to encounters with the living Christ that will change us utterly. A transforming community is one that, by its very nature, will be concerned with identifying concrete ways in which we can engage in life-transforming encounters with the real presence of Christ. The outcome of such encounters is that we will be able to discern and do the will of God. "Do not be conformed to this world, but be transformed by the renewing of your minds, *so that* you may discern what is the will of God—what is good and acceptable and perfect" (Romans 12:2, emphasis added).

PUTTING CHRIST BACK IN COMMUNITY

Certainly most Christians would give mental assent to the idea of gathering with other Christians in order to further the transformation process. It certainly sounds like the right thing to say and a worthy goal! The most important thing we need to understand deep in our souls that Christian community—*transforming* community—is not something we create or bring about by human effort. It is not an ideal that exists primarily in our own imaginations and vision. The community we are seeking already exists *in Christ* at the cosmic level (Colossians 1:15-20), and all we can do is find ways to open up to that reality and live it. This is very hopeful, if we will let it be. A great burden is relieved as we realize that this community is breathed into life through the Holy Spirit of Christ, not by anything we ourselves can take credit for.

Transforming community is the body of Christ alive on the earth now through the presence of the Holy Spirit. Each word we might use to describe the kind of community we are talking about here is useful in highlighting a different nuance, a different facet, of the beautiful diamond we call community. *Christian* highlights the person of Christ and what it might mean to live Christianly. *Transforming* emphasizes our commitment to being transformed in Christ's presence through concrete practices for opening to him. *Spiritual* highlights the work of the Holy Spirit in mediating Christ's presence in all the ways he promised.

> *Christian community is not an ideal which we must realize; it is rather a reality created by God in Christ in which we may participate.... The more genuine and the deeper our community becomes, the more will everything else between us recede, and the more clearly and purely will Jesus Christ and his work become the one and only thing that is vital between us. We have one another only through Christ, but through Christ we do have one another, wholly, and for all eternity.*
>
> Dietrich Bonhoeffer

Christian community. Transforming community. Spiritual community. Consider what each of these phrases means and what they mean to you. Use them all and use them well. Plumb their depths. Let them call your little group of companions to the single focus and yet all the multifaceted ways we journey together on the road between the now and the not yet. Lean in to the conversations that can take place when companions choose to walk together on the Emmaus Road—conversations in which Jesus himself draws near and we, too, find ourselves changed in his presence.

———————— ON THE ROAD TOGETHER ————————

Hopefully everyone in your group has taken time to read and reflect on the chapter in preparation for your gathering. You may want to agree on a facilitator who will open in prayer, watch the clock so you end at the agreed-upon time, and keep an eye out to be sure everyone has a chance to share. The role of facilitator can be alternated from meeting to meeting.

1. Share your responses to the descriptions at the beginning of the chapter: What thoughts, images and experiences come to mind when you think of community? Have you had an experience of your wish dream getting shattered? How has that affected you? How do you feel now about that experience? Have you worked through it to a place of inner resolution, able to see God's meaning in it? What else might be needed for you to experience what Bonhoeffer describes as "the salutary benefit" of having had a wish dream shattered?

2. Read Luke 24:13-35 out loud together. Where do you experience yourself to be on the road between the now and not yet? What is your first inclination when you find yourself on your own Emmaus Road—to seek out spiritual companions who can walk the road with you or to take the journey alone?

3. How do you respond to the idea of walking the road between the now and the not yet with these others? (Be sure to listen to and receive one another's sharing on this question without trying to fix, problem solve or give advice. Just receive each person's sharing as the gift of themselves that it is.)

4. How do you respond to the definition of transforming community as *men and women gathered around the presence of Christ in order to be transformed in Christ's presence so they can discern*

and do the will of God? What kind of desire does this stir up in you? (Make sure everyone responds to this question so you know where you are as a group.)

A PRAYER FOR WELCOMING CHRIST INTO OUR COMMUNITY

(The facilitator can lead the group by praying the entire prayer, or the facilitator can read the lowercase and the whole group read the uppercase together.)

Lord Jesus, stay with us,

FOR EVENING IS AT HAND AND THE DAY IS PAST;

Be our companion in the way, kindle our hearts and
    awaken hope,

THAT WE MAY KNOW YOU AS YOU ARE REVEALED IN
SCRIPTURE AND IN THE BREAKING OF BREAD.

Grant this for the sake of your love.

AMEN.

AND JESUS HIMSELF CAME NEAR

Welcoming the Stranger

*While they were talking and discussing, Jesus himself
came near and went with them, but their eyes were
kept from recognizing him. And he said to them,
"What are you discussing with each other
while you walk along?"*

LUKE 24:15-17

I am not very good at welcoming strangers. Truth be told, on most days I just don't feel the need for more relationships and would rather stick with the intimate few. I am sure this is due in part to my introverted nature and also the fact that my relational world seems very full. The other part of the truth is that some strangers are, well, *stranger* than others, which makes things just plain uncomfortable. I seem to have the ability to walk into a room and sense immediately who is the strangest of them all so I can then avoid the whole situation. I am not proud of this; I am just sayin'...

I remember one time in particular when I became acutely aware of my aversion to strangers and what I almost missed because of it. The context for this uncomfortable self-revelation was a two-year spiritual direction training program I participated in quite a while ago. Going into it, I knew the program included a small group component, and I was quite concerned about who I would be placed with. As I walked into our first residency, it didn't take long for me to become aware of who "the stranger" was for me.

At our first gathering we sat in a circle and introduced ourselves to one another. Immediately I noticed one woman who was somewhat peculiar, and that impression only worsened over time. For one thing, she came across as being very forward—pushy, even—and had a tendency to move too close and too quickly into one's personal space. I did not like that. She said things that were inappropriate and socially awkward, which made me feel nervous and uncomfortable. There were certain aspects of self-care that were obviously missing, and that really bothered me. On top of all that, she had lived her whole life as a cloistered nun, so I was convinced she would not be able to relate to my life as a married person, mother of three, on staff at a very large, very busy Protestant church. I *really* did not want to be in her group, so *of course* we were put in the same small group.

ANOTHER INCONVENIENT TRUTH

Being in a small group with this "stranger" was hard the whole way along. I never did enjoy it or get comfortable with it, and two years is a long time. But wouldn't you know, the most important, insightful thing that was said to me in the entire two years of participation in that group was said by this stranger—the person I never did really like, the person I never did get used to, the person I resisted most of the time. Again, I am not proud of this. I am not proud of my resistance to her, my prejudices and my intolerance of her "differentness." And yet here is another inconvenient truth of the spiritual life—that those who welcome the stranger into their conversations, their homes, their hearts and their lives have entertained angels without knowing it (Hebrews 13:2).

Just think—if the disciples on the Emmaus Road had refused to welcome the stranger into their companionable walk and their no-holds-barred conversation, they would have missed the whole mind-and spirit-bending encounter with Jesus! Even though it seemed like this was no time for strangers, it was while they were discussing "all these things that had happened" that a stranger approached them and asked a simple question: "What are you discussing with each other while you walk along?" *How rude!* we might think. *How socially inappropriate it is to walk up to two people who are having an intimate conversation and ask them right out what they are talking about.*

I don't know about you, but this is definitely the kind of strangeness I don't like. When I am with a close friend sharing things of a personal nature, the last thing I want to do is include someone neither one of us knows. It makes things awkward at best. At worst, it feels downright intrusive. But could it be that the stranger who intrudes on our life with such "otherness" has actually been sent by God as a means of grace?

One of the dynamics of transforming community is that there is enough "otherness" in the group that we can actually be challenged to stretch and grow beyond the confines of our own limited view of things and find ways to open to Christ as he is uniquely present in the other. In affinity groups, by contrast, there often isn't enough "otherness" to call forth anything new. If we don't venture outside our comfort zones, trusting that the stranger God has brought into our lives has something for us, we will never even know what we're missing.

For Personal Reflection

Reflect on a time recently when you had the opportunity to welcome a stranger or someone who was strange to you in some way. How did you feel? How did you respond?

STRANGE IN A GOOD WAY

Whatever the two disciples might have felt about being approached by a total stranger, Jesus had no qualms about joining them and including himself in their conversation. His apparently innocent inquiry invited them to share their story with him even though he, of all people, knew the story from the inside out! Like most of us, these two disciples found it hard to tell a stranger about something that had affected them so deeply; all they could do was stand still, mute with grief, looking sad. And this gracious stranger didn't try to rush them out of their grief, didn't force them beyond what they were able, didn't try to manage the moment. Instead, he stood right there with them in their sadness. He left the space open for them to experience all that they were feeling and gave them time to try and find the words.

Finally, Cleopas got a little exasperated. He gave up trying to put what he was experiencing into words and blurted out, "Are you the only stranger in Jerusalem who does not know the things that have taken place there in these days?" It is a bit like asking a US citizen, "Are you the only one who doesn't know what happened here on 9/11? Are you the only one who doesn't know about the airplanes and the World Trade Center and the Pentagon and the loss of life?" It's unthinkable that someone could be that out of touch with what's going on in the world!

Jesus' apparent lack of knowledge of the situation must have made him seem even stranger, but he continued to play dumb for a little while longer. "What things?" he asked, very simply. He seemed to know that they needed to tell their story, to get it all out in the presence of someone who knew how to listen. He knew that if they would just talk about it with him honestly, he could eventually help them find meaning in all that they had been through. So it all came pouring out—the pain, the grief, the disillusionment, the questions, the lost hopes and dreams. "*But we had hoped that he was the one to redeem Israel,*" they said. What a poignant statement about the depth of their loss and its far-reaching effect.

It was only after Jesus had taken time to listen deeply to their need—for comfort, for understanding, for perspective—that he offered any sort of perspective at all. And what he chose to do was draw them into the biblical story, interpreting Scriptures to them in such a way that all of it started to make sense. Masterfully, he helped them to locate their own story in the context of the larger story of God's redemptive purposes in the world. What seemed so hopeless from a human point of view was now imbued with profound spiritual significance. This "stranger" was quickly becoming a friend, and more than just a friend—a spiritual companion with an uncanny ability to listen to their hearts' deepest longings and questions.

They Urged Him Strongly to Stay

What happens next is a little over the top by contemporary standards. It seems these disciples from Emmaus were so stirred by the quality of this stranger's presence and his uncanny insight that they didn't want their conversation to end. When Jesus acted like he was going to keep on walking, they urged him to get off at their exit and to stay with them—in their home!

Now it's one thing to have a conversation with a stranger in a public place; it's quite another to invite him or her right into your home. Who does that these days? Maybe you've noticed that, in general, inviting people into our homes doesn't happen nearly as often as it used to. Today we tend toward "the third place"—meeting for coffee at Starbucks or a meal at a restaurant after church—and maintain our homes almost as a private retreat. It is becoming increasingly rare that even *friends* cook and share meals in each other's homes—let alone inviting random strangers home for dinner on the spur of the moment!

There is no doubt that something has shifted in our culture. When I was growing up, we always—and I do mean always—had people to our home for dinner after church on Sundays, or we were invited to someone else's house. On the days dinner was at our house, my mother put a roast in the oven before we left for church in the morning; since it took about three hours to cook, it would be ready when we got home. For some reason we were always starving when we got home (what is it about going to church that makes one so hungry?), and the aromas that greeted us as we walked in the door made home seem like seventh heaven. Whether it was with planned company (like the guest preacher and his family) or visitors who had shown up at our church for the first time, Sunday was a day for sharing a meal and then sharing fellowship throughout the afternoon. Other church families did this as well, so sometimes we were those who received welcome. Staying together a little longer after the

Sunday service was our norm, and we always looked forward to it.

Since no one could afford to take whole families out to a restaurant, hospitality always involved a meal (or at least a snack or a cup of tea) in someone's home—sometimes with very simple fare. As a pastor's family, we were always functioning on a slim budget (as I look back on it now, I realize that by some standards we were actually poor), but that never stopped us. Three hours of slow cooking could transform an inexpensive cut of meat into savory fare, and extra potatoes and carrots thrown in made up for whatever was lacking. The houses we lived in were always very modest, but no one seemed to care; it felt so good and soul satisfying to have fellowship over a meal in someone's home that the trappings didn't seem to matter. What mattered was the fact that friends and strangers who were about to become friends were together in someone's home.

As I reflect on these images from my growing-up years, they seem somewhat quaint, relics of a bygone era. And yet it wasn't that long ago that my husband and I, as a young married couple, followed in the footsteps of those hospitable families that had gone before. Less than one generation ago we, too, made it a priority of our young married life to invite folks for a meal in our first tiny apartment and later on our little starter home. But the cultural shifts have affected us as well. We do still invite people into our home occasionally, but these days, for a whole host of reasons, it seems easier to opt for the local coffee shop or a nearby restaurant as the optimal setting in which to spend time with people.

For Personal Reflection

What shifts have you noticed about the role of hospitality and welcome in your particular culture, age range, demographic? How do you feel about that?

INTIMATE INVITATIONS

No doubt there are significant sociological reasons for the changes in how and where people gather in our culture today. People are busy, urban settings seem more dangerous, and the exhaustion that results from our busyness lends itself to driving straight into the garage and entering our home or apartment without even acknowledging our neighbors. I am guilty of this myself.

Perhaps even more significant than cultural trends is the fact that inviting someone into our home for a meal is a whole lot more intimate than having a cup of coffee at Starbucks. When we invite people into our home, they see what we want them to see, and more! They see our family photos ("Hmm . . . you never mentioned you had a sister; what's your relationship like?") and memorabilia that points to the story of our lives ("I never knew you were a cheerleader/football player/trombone player!"). They see our tastes in decorating and are privy to what's finished and what's unfinished in our home. They experience the dynamics of our family life as children come and go and spouses interact in the process of cooking, setting the table and doing dishes together. Invited guests will see the books on our bookshelf, the magazines on our coffee table and evidence of our hobbies and interests. And if we're fortunate, we might all share the intimacy of preparation and cleanup—learning where to find the silverware and figuring out how the dishwasher gets loaded.

Unless we are masters at hiding, guests will leave our homes with a heightened "felt sense" of who we are and what we value. From the perspective of transforming community, this is a *really* good thing, because transforming community develops, in part, as we are willing to know and be known. As Henri Nouwen writes,

> I have many memories of encounters with people who made my heart burn but whom I did not invite into my home.

Sometimes it happens on a long plane trip, sometimes in a train, sometimes at a party. Afterwards I say to my friends, "Let me tell you whom I met today. A quite fascinating person. He said things so remarkable that I couldn't believe what I heard . . . I wish you could have met him! But he went on to . . . I don't know where!" Interesting, stimulating, and inspiring as all these strangers may be, when I do not invite them into my home, nothing truly happens. . . . Only with an invitation to "come and stay with me" can an interesting encounter develop into a transforming relationship.[1]

The whole experience of welcoming people into our homes can also foster important self-awareness—the kind that leads to further transformation. We do well to notice how we feel about opening our home to others. Is it something we anticipate with joy? Does it cause anxiety? Are we comfortable letting others see our lives pretty much as they are, or are there things we want to hide? Does opening our home become an occasion for running around frantically doing home improvements, or are we basically comfortable sharing what we have just as it is right now?

Paying attention to these inner dynamics can tell us about ourselves. How comfortable am I with myself and my life as God has given it to me right now? Is there an invitation to spiritual transformation contained within the practice of welcoming "the stranger" that has to do with cultivating contentment or greater comfort with lack of pretense? Is there a nudge (or even a push) to move beyond image management? Is there an invitation to further my understanding of true hospitality as opposed to mere "entertaining"? Can I use this as an opportunity to curb my perfectionism just a bit? Does contemplating hospitality and welcome help me become more aware of how I try to hide my real self with others?

How might these inner dynamics affect my participation in transforming community?

For Personal Reflection

Take a moment to stop here and reflect on the questions above—seriously and thoughtfully—in reference to past and recent times when others extended hospitality to you and you extended hospitality to others. Give some thought to how these inner dynamics might affect your ability to participate in transforming community with the community (or communities) you are a part of.

ENTERTAINING ANGELS

Providing hospitality and welcome to friends and strangers is consistently highlighted in Scripture as a Christian practice. When the writer of Hebrews says, "Do not neglect to show hospitality to strangers, for by doing that some have entertained angels without knowing it" (13:2), she or he is alluding to a very interesting story found in Genesis 18. While living on the backside of the desert, Abraham and Sarah extended generous hospitality to three strangers, only to discover later on that they were angels in disguise. Their example became the Old Testament standard for the Christian practice of welcoming the stranger. As if that were not enough, Jesus takes it one step further in Matthew 25:42-46 and points out that when we welcome all types of strangers we are welcoming Christ himself—which is exactly what happened to the two disciples on the Emmaus Road. They welcomed the stranger and then discovered it was Christ. Literally.

St. Benedict took Jesus' teaching so literally that when he wrote his Rule for how monks should live together in community, he gave specific instructions for how guests were to be treated with this truth in mind.

> Any guest who happens to arrive at the monastery should be received just as we would receive Christ himself, because he promised that on the last day he will say: I was a stranger and you welcomed me. . . . Guests should always be treated with respectful reverence. Those attending them both on arrival and departure should show this by a bow of the head or even a full prostration on the ground which will leave no doubt that it is indeed Christ who is received and venerated in them.[2]

I don't know about you, but however warmly I have greeted strangers, I have never bowed or prostrated myself. Yet the more literally one takes Jesus' statement that when we welcome "the least of these" we welcome him, the more the idea of bowing and genuflecting makes sense!

We seem to have a choice: either we can avoid the intimacy of fully welcoming "the other" or we can lean into it, knowing that extending this kind of welcome is another step toward fostering the transforming community we seek. In fact, the choice to open our homes to one another is so countercultural today that it might be as significant as choosing what book or Bible study we will engage together! After all, it was during an ordinary, spur-of-the-moment meal in someone's ordinary home that the disciples' eyes were opened and they recognized the fact that this "stranger" was no stranger at all!

Perhaps it could be that way for us as well. Perhaps in the ordinariness of sharing a meal or a cup of coffee *in one another's space* we can truly recognize each other as fellow human beings with cares and concerns, loves and hates, finished and unfinished business—just like us! Perhaps in the context of such ordinariness, our "strangeness" to one another can be transformed into spiritual companionship as the light of Jesus' indwelling presence is revealed in every face.

STRANGE FRIENDS, INTIMATE STRANGERS

The Emmaus story raises an interesting question: Who is the stranger, really? Is it always the immigrant or the foreigner or the poor person on the street? Sometimes it is one of these, to be sure, and finding ways to offer meaningful welcome to these "strangers" is a life-changing practice on many levels—personal, communal and global. On a global level, immigration is a significant contemporary issue that, for Christians at least, must be considered through the lens of the biblical emphasis on hospitality and welcome and treating others as we would like to be treated. "When an alien resides with you in your land, you shall not oppress the alien. The alien who resides with you shall be to you as the citizen among you; you shall love the alien as yourself, for you were aliens in the land of Egypt: I am the LORD your God" (Leviticus 19:33-34). Wow! That's pretty direct!

More often than not, however, the stranger is simply someone who is strange *to you* or different *from you* for one reason or another—a personality type that is different from yours, different life experiences, a different ethnicity, a different opinion or perspective on an important topic, or even just a different life stage. It could be someone who seems to come out of nowhere, interrupting your normal re-

> The Emmaus story reveals to us the image of a God and a church that walk alongside human confusion, human pain, and human loss of faith and hope. Emmaus challenges us to see that it isn't our unshakeable faith and deep spirituality that connect us with the risen Christ, but our smallest gestures of hospitality and friendship.
>
> Amy Hunter

lating patterns or intruding upon your established circle of friends. It might be someone who doesn't fit in or simply rubs you the wrong way. The question is, can we welcome the one who is strange in *that* way? How can we be as receptive to Christ *in them* as those two despairing disciples were open and receptive to Jesus on the Emmaus Road? What we are really talking about here is being willing to welcome diversity, in the broadest sense of the word, and receiving the gifts that come through such diversity.

The Emmaus story teaches us not to make too much of a distinction between who's strange and who's not, because it's probably only a matter of degree. At any moment a stranger can become a friend, or a friend can become someone we don't even recognize. When it comes to friends and strangers, we don't always know which is which. The little community that developed on the road to Emmaus was made up of two friends and a stranger who eventually became a friend. Neither of the friends who started out together had the missing piece of insight and information that would make sense of it all. Only the "stranger" could bring that. We never know which stranger will have the insight or the perspective or the loving gesture that will strengthen the community we already have and unlock the meaning we are looking for.

In order to receive what "the other" has to give, we will need to practice what

Creator of the world, eternal God,
we have come from many places for
a little while.

Redeemer of humanity, God-with-us,
we have come with all our differences,
seeking common ground.

Spirit of unity, go-between God,
we have come on journeys of our own,
to a place where journeys meet.

So let us take time together,
for when paths scross and pilgrims gather,
there is much to share and celebrate.
Amen.

Iona Abbey Worship Book

I call *inner hospitality*—that is, a spirit of openness and receptivity to those unlikely moments when the friendliness of a stranger or the strangeness of a friend causes our hearts to burn within us. We will need to learn new ways of being in conversation that honor and care for the more tender aspects of our lives—which will be the subject of the next chapter.

WELCOMING CHRIST IN YOU

Recently, I had another amazing experience of welcoming and being enriched by "the other." It was a retreat on the subject of honoring the body as a spiritual discipline, and at the outset I made the statement that we would discuss gender as a fundamental "in the body" experience but due to limited time, we would not be dealing with the issue of race even though it, too, is an important aspect of life in the body. My decision made perfect sense to me (of course!), but at the break, a black pastor approached me very graciously and let me know that he did not resonate with my statement. In fact, he said, he considered race to be more defining than gender, for when he enters a room, he is always much more aware of his race than of his gender. Immediately I knew that I needed to be more careful about making my experience the measure of all things.

After we talked for a few minutes, I asked him if he would be willing to share the difference he had named with the entire group and lead us in a conversation that would move us beyond being strangers to one another in this regard. He agreed, so we adjusted our schedule to include a conversation about this difference. In a gracious and thoughtful way he described some of his experiences as a black male—experiences that those in the room who are white had never had and really needed to hear about. Eventually others in the group added their voices. Another pastor shared her experiences of being black and female—which was, in significant ways, different from being a black male. Then an Asian man spoke quietly of his struggle for self-acceptance in the midst of prevailing cultural stereotypes, and a Latino man offered his perspective as well. What was spoken was so compelling that at times the whole group fell silent out of respect for the significance of what was being shared.

There we all were—strangers to one another in ways we didn't fully realize, until we were able to welcome that which was different in the other with honesty, love and respect. A sense of profound intimacy descended upon the group as a white woman, a black man, a black woman, an Asian man, a Latino and all those looking on welcomed "the other" by entering in and allowing ourselves to be affected by one another's experience. Jesus himself came near, deepening our care and commitment to one another, along with our concern for a more just society. I had a sense that it was only the beginning of the transforming work God wants to do in us as we continued to welcome each other in all of our strangeness. I was convinced that if we could see our "otherness" *as a gift*, rather than a problem or an inconvenience, we would all be changed for the better.

On a purely human level, welcoming the stranger still doesn't always come naturally. But I can tell you that my experience with the cloistered nun all those years ago has changed me right up to this day. I am never able to encounter a stranger without wondering, "Is this the person through whom God is going to speak? Is this the stranger who is going to be Christ to me today?" What I know now is that the practice of welcoming the stranger opens me to the presence of Christ in the most unexpected places—it changes me in very good ways—and *that* is something I don't want to miss.

————————— ON THE ROAD TOGETHER —————————

For Discussion: As you reflect on the way in which the whole Emmaus Road encounter hinged on the disciples' willingness to welcome the stranger, spend time considering the make-up of your group. In what areas do you experience sameness, natural affinity and feeling known by one another?

In what areas do you experience your "strangeness" to one another—in other words, areas in which you are different from one another or where there is some diversity of race, gender, life experience or current life stage, difference of opinion? Is there a place in yourself where you don't feel particularly known or understood within the group, or an aspect of someone else's life or situation that is unknown to you?

What would it look like for you to welcome one another and experience each other as a gift in these areas? What transformative possibilities are contained simply within the makeup of your group?

For Practice: Consider sharing at least one meal or refreshments in each person's home, using the visit as an opportunity for that person to further share themselves and important aspects of their lives. If members of your group live in the same neighborhood, you could do a progressive dinner (appetizers at one home, dinner at another home, dessert at another); if you are more spread out, you can go from one home to the next over a period of weeks or months. These times in each other's homes will help you get to know each other's lives—learning more about family history and life experiences through family photos, sharing hobbies and passions like cooking or wine tasting, perhaps engaging in a recreational activity like a pool party or a campfire or a volleyball game. Use this as a chance to get to know one another in a more fully orbed way than is possible when you just sit around or meet for coffee at a Starbucks, and see what happens!

A Prayer for Welcoming the Stranger

Stay with us, Lord,
since the day is far spent and the night is coming:
kindle our hearts on the way, that we may recognize you in
    the Scriptures,
in the breaking of the bread, and in each other.
As the poor widow welcomed Elijah,
let us be open to the richness and miracle in meeting.
As Abraham and Sarah welcomed passing strangers,
let us entertain the possibility of angels in disguise.
Let our eyes be opened, that we may recognize in our neighbor
the divine presence of Christ.
AMEN.[3]

3

THEY STOOD STILL
LOOKING SAD

Choosing to Listen Rather Than Fix

*They stood still, looking sad. Then one of them, whose name
was Cleopas, answered him, "Are you the only stranger
in Jerusalem who does not know the things that
have taken place there in these days?"
He asked them, "What things?"*

LUKE 24:17-19

This particular moment on the Emmaus Road is one that causes me to fall in love with Jesus all over again. You've gotta love a man (or a woman) who asks a good question, waits patiently for you to sort through your thoughts and emotions, and then asks a follow-up question that finally helps you to say what you need to say. Spiritual conversation just doesn't get any better than that!

Jesus models for us here another important element of transforming community—the ability to simply listen and *be with what is* without having to fix, give advice or problem solve. He seemed to know that what these two disoriented disciples needed, first of all, was to tell the story of what had happened and how it affected them in their own words. Even though Jesus definitely would have had his own perspective, he didn't rush in and offer that too quickly. He respected the fact that their experience of these events, the meanings they were placing on it all and the questions they were asking in response were their own. What they needed was someone who would simply listen and be present to them in all their pain and uncertainty.

Yet even when we are graciously given such an opportunity to speak, it is not always easy to talk about traumatic personal events. Cleopas and the unnamed disciple struggled to come up with the words that would adequately express what they were experiencing, but they couldn't, so they finally just gave up and gave in to their sadness.

Have you ever been in a situation where what you were going through was so awful or so wonderful you couldn't find words to describe it? Were you blessed to be around people who knew how to "stand still, looking sad" with you, or did you have to endure inane comments that missed the point or advice that added insult to injury?

If you're the listener in a moment like this, one of the greatest temptations is to rush in and fill up the emptiness with words—

of advice ("What really helped me when I lost my job was . . ."), well-meaning attempts at comfort ("I know exactly how you feel"), or filler ("I'm sure God has a plan"). Such words are intended mostly to relieve the awkwardness we ourselves are feeling; they are rarely what the person who is in the throes of pain or upheaval really needs. Why do we do this? I suppose the obvious answer is that we really do want to help. It is difficult to witness another person's pain, and if we have any goodness in our heart at all, we want to somehow alleviate it or at least bring some sort of meaning and comfort.

The dark side of these good intentions, however, is that we might also have a bit of a messiah complex. On some level, we might relish the opportunity to be the savior of the world, or at least the savior of the person who is sitting in pain right in front of us. We would like to be the one who has the word that brings needed comfort or the advice that solves the problem. Some of us are actually addicted to "helping" because it make us feel better about ourselves. Or we are so fundamentally self-focused that we really cannot let someone else's experience be their own without somehow making it about us—our own story, what we think we know, what we feel we can contribute to their situation.

THE POWER OF PRESENCE

Transforming community begins as we choose to walk together, trusting that Jesus is in our midst as we talk and share about "all these things that had happened." But it doesn't end there. Transforming community continues to unfold and deepen among us as we ask good questions and learn how to stand still and wait with one another in the midst of shattered hopes and dreams and the great unfixables of life. There is a quality of listening and being together with Jesus in the stuff of our lives that can open us to fresh

perspectives and true spiritual insight, or at the very least an ability
to let go and lean in to the situation just as it is.

I remember one experience with our youngest daughter, Haley,
that continues to remind me of the power of this kind of listening
and being with. It was Christmas Day, and she was ten years old.
We had invited some dear family friends to join us for Christmas
dinner, and everyone was looking forward to a wonderful day together. The only problem was that Haley had contracted pneu-
monia, and our friends had twins who had been born prematurely
and could not risk being exposed to an infection. For several days
leading up to Christmas, we watched and hoped and prayed that
Haley would get better, but it was not meant to be. Our plans had
to be canceled, and Haley was devastated; she had been looking
forward to the day so much, and she also felt responsible for "ru-
ining everyone's Christmas."

After the final decision was made, she ran up to her room crying.
I followed her, desperately wanting to be able to fix things somehow
or make it all better—as all parents long to do when their children
are hurting. But there was nothing that would alleviate this pain;
it could only be endured. And all I could do was sit there with her
on the bed, stroking her hair as she cried into my lap. We stayed
like that for a while, and then I did have to go downstairs and work
on Christmas dinner, trusting God to do something for her that I
could not do. About a half an hour later she came downstairs and
found me in the kitchen, wrapped her arms around my waist and
said, "Thanks, Mom, for sitting with me. I feel better now."

It was that simple and that hard. What most needed to be
done in her heart only God could do. I felt like I hadn't done
anything. But it turned out that the simple presence of another
human being who could be with her in the pain was part of how
God ministered to her.

> ### *For Personal Reflection*
>
> When have you experienced something so deep that you needed someone to just be present with you rather than rushing in to try to fix, problem solve, give advice? Did you have people who were able to do that? What did that mean to you? What difference did it make? Have you ever had an experience with someone who really was not able to do that? How did that affect you?

counseling skills

THE SERVICE OF LISTENING

The Emmaus Road narrative invites us to consider the practice of Christlike listening as one aspect of our commitment to transforming community. Bonhoeffer points out,

> The first service one owes to others in the fellowship consists in listening to them. . . . It is God's love to us that He not only gives us His Word but also lends us His ear. . . . Christians so often think they must always contribute something when they are in the company of others, that this is the one service they have to render. They forget that listening can be a greater service than speaking.[1]

While the practice of listening might seem a little "soft" and ill-defined when compared to more traditional small group practices such as Bible study, prayer and service, it helps to remember that the context for Bonhoeffer's observation was Christian brothers suffering together in a German concentration camp. Clearly this was a place where easy answers and superficial sentimentality would not do, but "the greater service" of true listening was most highly valued. Bonhoeffer drives the point home even further:

He who can no longer listen to his brother will soon be no longer listening to God either; he will be doing nothing but prattle in the presence of God, too. . . . One who cannot listen long and patiently will presently be talking beside the point and be never really speaking to others, albeit he be not conscious of it.[2]

Kids

For Personal Reflection

How do you respond to the idea that "listening can be a greater service than speaking"? How often do you serve others in this way?

PRESENT TO GOD ON BEHALF OF OTHERS

Transforming community involves cultivating a kind of spiritual companionship that is very different from what we usually experience. It involves being present to the person we are listening to, yes, but even more importantly *being present to God on the other's behalf.* We are listening for what God's desire or guidance for that person might be, not what our best advice might be or how we can be most helpful. Furthermore, we are willing to be made aware of what is going on within ourselves so that our own inner urges (to fix, problem solve, alleviate discomfort) don't get in the way of what God wants to do in the moment.

I look at God, I look at you, and I keep looking at God.

Julian of Norwich

This quality of presence can also be described as an *intercessory prayer stance*. The problem is that many of us have experienced intercession to be so effortful and exhausting that the word itself scares us away. However, the Scriptures assure us that it is the Holy Spirit who does the real work anyway—continually interceding for the saints (that would be us!) with groans too deep for words (Romans 8:26). Thus spiritual companionship can be understood as prayerful listening in which we remain quiet enough to listen for the prayer of the Holy Spirit that is already being prayed for that person before the throne of grace. We can ask God to give us some sense of what the Holy Spirit is already praying so we can participate in that prayer in whatever way God leads.

When asked by a friend how she prayed for others, Julian of Norwich described such prayerful companionship this way: "I look at God, I look at you, and I keep looking at God." What Julian is describing is a very freeing way to listen and be present to others. "Looking at God" (or Jesus) speaks to the idea that even before I start listening to another person, I can acknowledge the reality that both of us are in God's presence. I can pray that I will be sensitized to God's purposes in this person's life and in our conversation rather than being swayed by my own agenda. Then as I "look at you" and listen to you, I am not seeing you or experiencing our interaction simply in human terms. I am "listening through" to sense God's heart and God's prayer for you so that I can join God in that prayer. I am aware of myself and the other in God's presence, desiring only to be responsive to whatever God is doing in the moment.

Being aware of myself in God's presence means that I am also willing to be made conscious of my own inner dynamics, so I can be wise and refuse to allow anything that is going on within me to get in the way of what God might be doing. It means I am willing to set aside anything that might keep me from being fully present to God on the other's behalf. So for instance, if someone is sharing something wonderful that is going on in his or her life—a promotion, an unexpected opportunity, some experience that is full of joy and satisfaction—I might notice that it makes me feel a little jealous or competitive, and I am able to ask God to help me set aside feelings of jealousy in order to celebrate what God is doing.

Or perhaps someone is sharing a life experience that is similar to something I have experienced, and I become aware that I run the risk of projecting my own story and my own feelings onto them. When, by God's grace, I am aware of my own inner tendencies, I can ask God to help me set aside my projections in order to be fully present to what that person is experiencing and what God might be saying to them. This might be very different from how I would experience it or what God would say to me in a similar situation. As I cultivate such self-awareness, I might become aware of how uncomfortable I am with tears, strong emotions or complicated life situations and can choose to resist the urge to say something—anything!—in order to alleviate that discomfort. I might even become aware of how I use humor to avoid being present with myself and others in the midst of the great unfixables of life.

"Looking at God again" means that once I have listened to the other person, I don't have to rush in with my own thoughts and words. Just as Jesus did with the disciples on the Emmaus Road, I can be still with that person and allow my silence to express reverent attention to what they have just shared. As I am present to God on the other's behalf, God may give a word to speak, a prayer to pray, a loving act to offer—or he may not. It could be that there are no words and we are guided to be silent with the other, allowing the Holy Spirit to pray with and for us as we are quietly together.

As you can see, this is very different from the problem solving, advice giving and attempts at bringing human comfort that often happen when Christian people get together. This kind of listening creates and protects a space between us that is hospitable to the soul—a place where it becomes safe enough to speak of our hopes and dreams, our longings and desires. In his book *A Hidden Wholeness*, Parker Palmer shares about a time when he was going through depression. He says, "When I went into a deadly darkness that I had to walk alone, the darkness called clinical depression, I took comfort and drew strength from those few people who neither fled from me nor tried to save me but were simply present to me."[3]

Palmer's comments highlight one of the great paradoxes of human experience: in the deepest experiences of our lives—birth, death, depression, loss, calling, spiritual longing and desire—we are profoundly alone. And yet there is something we as human beings *can* offer one another in the midst of that existential loneliness—the gift of our presence. Perhaps one of the reasons "simple presence" between human beings is so powerful is that it creates space in which the Ultimate Presence can be experienced as the Voice that speaks, the Love that comforts and the Fullness that fills all emptiness.

LISTENING LIKE JESUS

Spiritual friendship and companionship characterized by this kind of intercessory prayer stance is at the heart of transforming community precisely because it creates so much space for listening to God in Christ through the ministry of the Holy Spirit. One writer describes this kind of companionship as "listening the other into free speech." I have pondered this phrase for a long time, for it strikes me as being so true and yet so hard to come by in the circles in which most of us live and work and fellowship. The author, Mary Sharon Moore, defines free speech not so much as a human right but as "an abiding interior freedom to speak the truth of one's being . . . freedom to be heard and received, freedom to hear and receive God's calling in my life." She distinguishes free speech from empty speech (endless, mindless chatter that fills every pocket of silence), false speech (which reveals a disconnection between one's inner self and outer response and betrays one's inner truth) and unfree speech (which reveals a sense of victimhood with phrases like "I can't . . . ," I should . . . ," "I ought . . . ," "I have no choice . . .").

Conversely, free speech

reveals the authentic self-in-God. Spiritually free speech
honors the complexity and mystery of one's self and circumstances in life. In the presence of deep listening, the spiritually free person can speak the incongruence between one's
poverties and God's love, one's sinfulness and divine mercy,
one's small-heartedness and God's persistent generosity. Free
speech is the hallmark of the spiritually mature and maturing
person in the midst of spiritual paradox. Free speech reveals
an interior centeredness in God and freedom to participate
in the divine mystery as it unfolds in the course of one's life.[4]

This may be at least one aspect of the kind of speech Paul refers to
in Ephesians when he says, "Speaking the truth in love, we must
grow up in every way" (4:15).

This description of one who is free to speak authentically of
one's experience of God's presence (or seeming absence!) in the
midst of one's real-life situation strikes me as an apt reflection of
how Jesus listened the disciples into speech on the Emmaus
Road. Even though he certainly had his perspective on the situation (which he shared fruitfully later on), his initial invitation to
them was the complete freedom to tell it like it was for them. The
goal of such listening is to lovingly and humbly evoke the freedom
of others, to invite them into the fresh air and light of unjudged
and unafraid expressions of who they are in God. Indeed, spiritual companionship begins as together we embrace basic guidelines for this particular kind of listening rather than assuming
that we each know how.

Listening that evokes spiritually free speech in the other

- does not interrupt but rather creates space for the person to
discover and express what they need to say;

- refrains from using evaluative phrases such as "Oh, that's good" or "How terrible!"—responses that merely communicate how we feel about what they are sharing, rather than giving them the opportunity to describe in depth how they are responding;

- waits on what the Spirit desires to reveal rather than rushing in with one's own thoughts and interpretations;

- asks questions that continually seek to unlock the deeper reality of the other person's experience, gently offering them permission to explore, own and integrate their experiences into their spiritual experience—questions like "What was that like for you?" "How did you experience God (or not) in the midst of that experience?" "What happens when you pray about that?" "What questions does that raise for you?";

- encourages the person toward mature faith—in other words, to discover God's presence and trust God's purposes in all aspects of life (and they themselves have to discover it; we cannot force this kind of insight on them);

- invites the other into creative participation in God's redemptive purposes in the world: a greater connectedness with what God is doing in the world, a clearer sense of one's place in it, and a generous response to God's calling according to the gifts one has been given.[5]

As it turns out, this is exactly the kind of listening and speaking the disciples experienced on the Emmaus Road.

A LISTENING PRACTICE

Given just how countercultural this kind of listening is, most of us could use some kind of spiritual practice that helps us to, well, practice. Group spiritual direction is just such a practice; it provides a structure with concrete disciplines built in that help us to be the kind of spiritual companions we really want to be. For group spiritual direction, people gather on a regular basis to assist one another in being more attentive and responsive to God's presence in all of life. They meet to reflect on their spiritual journeys (the road between the now and the not yet), to notice Jesus' presence and activity in each other's lives through the real presence of the Holy Spirit, and to support one another in responding faithfully to that presence.

In group spiritual direction it is understood that the Holy Spirit is the true director and can work and speak by virtue of the fact that the group members enter into a shared discipline that creates space to listen. Rose Mary Dougherty has pioneered a well-defined approach to group spiritual direction, and she identifies three conditions as essential to the life of such a group. Members agree to

- commit themselves to an honest relationship with God;

- participate wholeheartedly in the group process through prayerful listening and response;

- open their spiritual journeys for consideration by others.[6]

One thing that distinguishes group spiritual direction from other kinds of group practice is the commitment to a very disciplined structure that holds the group to its shared intent. While several excellent comprehensive works on the practice of group spiritual direction are available,[7] I will offer a brief description here along with some simple instructions for how your group can use this discipline in whole or in part. You may want to practice it as a way of cultivating your ability to listen to one another as Jesus listened to the disciples on the Emmaus Road. Even if you don't feel up to incorporating the entire process into your group times, single elements can be introduced and practiced as appropriate. For instance, simply allowing people to share fully without interrupting them or introducing some silence into your group time will be highly beneficial to your ability to companion one another.

Typically a gathering for group spiritual direction will begin with silence—anywhere from three to even twenty minutes. During this silence participants orient themselves toward God and settle into their shared intent. Most groups benefit from having a designated facilitator or convener who simply holds the process in place by keeping time, indicating when a person is free to begin sharing, and calling the group back into silence after the "presenter" has finished. I have shortened the time frames from what the traditional practice recommends in order to accommodate larger groups or shorter time frames, but have noted both times for your consideration.

Opening silence (3-5 minutes)
You may want to begin the silence by lighting a candle as a symbol of the presence of the Holy Spirit, reminiscent of the tongues of fire in Acts 2. The convener closes the silence with "Come, Holy Spirit," or some other brief prayer that acknowledges the presence of Jesus through the Holy Spirit as the real director.

Sharing by one person—the "presenter" (5-7 minutes or 10-15 minutes)
The presenter shares an experience, a question or a matter for discernment while the group listens prayerfully through to the end, without interruption.

Silence (3-4 minutes)
This silence makes space for God, allowing God to expose anything within that would prevent group members from being present to this person and their story, and listening for the prayer of the Holy Spirit for this person (Romans 8:26-28). Each member might also ask, "God, is there anything you want me to offer this person out of my prayer?"

Response from companions (3-5 minutes or about 10 minutes)
This is a period of sharing the questions, comments or images that have come up in the silence. The convener may want to remind people that they can trust God's caring love for the presenter and that God's love can be active in both silence and words. Companions can demonstrate trust for the group process by moving with the flow of the group rather than holding on to a personal agenda or any need to offer what has come to them if it feels inconsistent with where the Spirit is leading the group as a whole. During this move, members should be careful to adhere to the listening guidelines delineated earlier in this chapter.

Silence (1-2 minutes or about 5 minutes)
This time of silence is to give the presenter an opportunity to "gather up" what she or he has received, to listen for what seemed to be from the Holy Spirit, most helpful or clarifying, et cetera, and what didn't seem to fit. The presenter may even want to take a few notes to capture what they have received in order to be fully present to the next presenter. During this time, the rest of the group prays for the person who has just presented, holding them in God's loving presence with confidence that the One who has begun a good work in them will bring it to completion.

At first glance, this process might seem odd or even awkward, and it certainly is different from the kinds of sharing groups most of us are used to. However, after years of training, participating in and facilitating such groups, I would affirm this practice as one of the most profound ways a group can open itself to the real presence of the Holy Spirit, who mediates the loving, guiding, companioning presence of Jesus himself. Surprising things are shared, amazing insights are received, and we experience ourselves to be part of something more than mere human companionship.

———————— ON THE ROAD TOGETHER ————————

In chapter one you had the opportunity to share where you were experiencing yourself to be on the road between the now and the not yet. This time you will have the opportunity to share this a little bit more fully and to actually companion one another in that place on your journey. Choose a convener to watch the clock.

Following the process outlined above (opening silence>>sharing by one person>>silence>>response from companions>>silence), give each person the opportunity to be the presenter, sharing where they are experiencing themselves to be on the road between the now and the not yet and how they are experiencing Jesus with them (or not) on that road. The difference between this time and last is that this sharing is not primarily for the sake of discussion but for the sake of spiritual companionship.

This time, you will practice the first three moves of the group spiritual direction process, which is a way of learning to simply be still and present to God for one another in silence after each one has shared. This is a very concrete way of practicing the intercessory prayer stance described in this chapter.

- "First I look at God." Begin with two to three minutes of opening silence. The facilitator will close the silence with a brief prayer such as "Come, Holy Spirit."

- "Then I look at you." The first person will then receive the undivided attention of the group as they "present" or share in a little more detail how and where they are experiencing themselves to be on the road between the now and the not yet.

- "Then I look at God again." When that person is finished sharing, the facilitator will invite the group into silence by saying something like, "Let's enter into silence to be present to God on _____'s behalf."

- After two to three minutes, the facilitator can affirm and bring closure to the presenter's experience by saying, "Thanks be to God."

The facilitator can go last with another member of the group guiding the process for them.

Don't worry about doing it just right; simply be willing to try, trusting God as you learn and practice together. Listening to four people is about all human beings can manage in one meeting. If your group is larger than four, use two meetings so everyone has the opportunity to present and be companioned in this way. You might want to begin by praying this prayer together.

A PRAYER FOR LISTENING IN COMMUNITY

Lord, we gather together this day [or night]
as openly and as honestly as we are presently able.

FOR THESE MOMENTS THAT ARE SANCTIFIED FOR
        LISTENING IN COMMUNITY,
MAY WE BE BLESSED TO KNOW THE GOODNESS OF GODLY
        COMPANY,
THE PACE OF GRACE LEADING US GENTLY,
AND THE LIFE OF YOUR REFRESHING SPIRIT
HOVERING OVER THE FACE OF THE WATERS OF OUR LIVES
READY AND WILLING TO BRING FORTH NEW LIFE
EVEN IN THE FORMLESS AND VOID PLACES OF OUR
HEARTS AND COMMUNITIES.
ENABLE US TO TRUST YOUR SPIRIT AMONG US
AS WE ARE PRESENT TO YOU ON BEHALF OF ONE ANOTHER,

for we are gathered in your strong name, Lord Jesus Christ.
Amen.[8]

But We Had Hoped . . .

Gathering on the Basis of Shared Desire

But we had hoped that he was the one to redeem Israel.

LUKE 24:21

One of the things Jesus seemed to love doing in spiritual conversation was to ask questions that helped people get in touch with what was deeply true for them. Whether it was good, bad or ugly, he preferred that they speak honestly rather than skate along the surface of things. His questions encouraged people to take the deeper dive and talk about their hopes and dreams, desires and disappointments. For Jesus, this was what it meant to be companions on the way, and the disciples on the Emmaus Road got there pretty quickly in their roadside exchange.

After expressing some exasperation with Jesus' apparent cluelessness, they recounted the basic facts of what happened in Jerusalem in fairly succinct terms. And then came that poignant phrase—*but we had hoped.* These words are simple and yet so profound—pregnant with all the longing and desire that had drawn their little community together in the first place. Over time that desire had blossomed into real hope and then deepened into full-blown faith that what they had allowed themselves to hope for was really going to happen. They had rearranged their lives and taken great risks in order to live into their desire for a new kind of kingdom, one that would be established through the coming of the long-awaited Messiah. Weary and disillusioned from living under Roman rule, they longed to be free to live under God's good rule. They had been so convinced that Jesus was indeed the Messiah who would usher in this new regime that they had staked their very lives on it.

At the same time, they seemed to be perpetually confused about exactly how this kingdom would come. They had been under the impression that Jesus was going to set up this new kingdom through some sort of military coup, not through an approach to power that involved death, burial and resurrection! Their group had coalesced around their shared desire for this new kingdom and their belief that Jesus could bring about the fulfillment of their deepest desire. And since they had "gotten in on the ground floor," they envisioned themselves in places of prominence in this new kingdom. So they had left their homes and their livelihoods to give allegiance to the teaching and vision of the One who had just been violently taken from them. If you think about it, most communities come together on the basis of some sort of shared vision or desire, and even when the reality isn't there, they still keep hoping that something good will come.

For Personal Reflection

When have you let yourself hope for something like the disciples did, only to have your hopes dashed? What have you done with that experience? Has it robbed you of the ability to hope now, or do you still allow yourself to hope?

Touching Desire in Community

Having our hopes dashed leaves us in a very tender place indeed. Having our hopes dashed means that at one time we had actually allowed ourselves to hope! We got in touch with something we really wanted, and we let it matter to us a great deal. As the possibility of achieving that desire became more and more real, it was more than just a dream; we could actually picture it, and we found ourselves leaning in and living as though that thing might really happen. Perhaps it even became the organizing principle of our lives. That's how desire works, and it is very powerful—much more powerful than oughts, shoulds and momentary inspirations.

Jesus understood this. He knew that if people got in touch with their true spiritual desires it would change their lives, so he encouraged them to pay attention to desire and then actually speak of it *out loud* in his presence! When two disciples of John started to follow Jesus, he turned to them and said, "What are you looking for?" (John 1:38). When Bartimaeus cried out to Jesus from the side of the Jericho road, Jesus asked, "What do you want me to do for you?" (Mark 10:51). When James and John marched into Jesus' presence announcing presumptuously, "We want you to do for us whatever we ask of you," Jesus graciously responded, "What is it you want me to do for you?" (Mark 10:35-36).

When Jesus approached the invalid at the pool of Beth-zatha, he actually upped the ante and asked, "Do you want to be made well?" (John 5:6). In other words, "How bad do you want it? Do you want it bad enough to get up and actually do something about it?"

"What do you want me to do for you?" is actually the question Jesus asked most frequently in the New Testament. He knew that being in touch with desire has the potential to shape decisions and affect the overall trajectory and outcomes of a person's life. Desire, rightly identified and effectively harnessed, eventually gives way to the *hope* that what we desire really could come to pass and the *faith* to live as though it were real. The spiritual journey deepens as we discover the longing and desires God has placed within us and that God himself longs to meet (Psalm 37:4). While we might think something as personal as desire originates with us, the truth is, everything of significance in the spiritual life originates with God—even our desire. We love God because God first loved us. We long for God because God first longed for us. We reach for God because God first reached for us. Hence we discover that God is there in the midst of our desire, drawing us to himself and to the life we were meant for.

With good attention, *desire* deepens into *intentionality*, which can then be lived out in the *decisions* we make every day. And that is where transforming community comes in. As we get in touch with our truest longings and desires, we need a community that can listen to our desire and support us in choosing practices and life rhythms that are congruent with what we say we want—intimacy with God, deeper levels of transformation in God's presence, soul friendship and connection with others, and the freedom and courage to offer the gifts of an authentic self to the world. One of the primary functions of spiritual community, or transforming community, is to listen to one another's spiritual desire and affirm God's presence and invitation in the midst of that desire so we can make choices that are congruent with it. Then we can support one another in responding faithfully with our life choices.

So here's how this works. Thirty-five-year-old Brent is married with three children—a son and two daughters—whom he adores. He is also a rising star in his company, which sells computer products and services. As he has gotten in touch with his desire, he is able to share with the group that even though his career is exciting, what he wants most in this life is to be a good dad and be there for his kids. His own father traveled a lot, and he remembers missing his dad profoundly during those absences. He also sees many colleagues who are sacrificing family for career, and deep in his heart he knows that if he gets to the end of his life and has missed the chance to fully receive the gift of family God has given him, he will have failed to live his deepest (and he believes, God-given) desires.

With great passion and even a few tears, Brent has shared this desire with his transforming community, and when they meet together, these spiritual companions have faithfully asked him how he is doing at living in ways that are congruent with his desires. How many hours did he work this last week? Was he able to be at his kids' sporting events? Was he rested enough to give them good attention, or was he distracted and exhausted? Their questions are not so much about accountability as about supporting him in living into his heart's deepest desire.

And then the inevitable happens. Brent is offered a promotion that would require a lot more travel. He is torn and seeking God's guidance. Without giving their opinions or offering advice, his spiritual companions are able to simply ask questions about how this promotion might affect his ability to live into the deepest desire of his heart. Brent is aware that, by God's grace, these companions are able to ask a whole different set of questions from those of his boss, his career coach or his golfing buddies, and he is grateful.

This is what transforming community exists for; this is what spiritual companions talk about and pay attention to when they get together. It is the kind of intentional relationship Thomas Merton is casting vision for when he says, "Ask me not where I live or what I like to eat . . . ask me what I think I am living for, in detail, and ask me what I think is keeping me from living fully for the thing I want to live for."[1]

DISCERNING DESIRE

We all have lots of desires, but not all desires are created equal. As Phillip Sheldrake explains,

> All desires are real experiences, [but] not all are equally authentic in the sense of being expressions of our authentic selves. Certain desires spring from a more profound level of ourselves than others. . . . Unless we feel free to own our desires in the first place, we will never learn how to recognize those that are more fruitful and healthy, let alone how to live out of the deepest desires of all. . . . The more honestly we try to identify our authentic desires, the more we can identify who we really are.[2]

Companions in transforming community can actually help us discern the true desires that lie beneath the more obvious ones like that next home improvement, the new car or the latest fashion. While we must be careful not to dismiss or negate the desires we are most conscious of, a willingness to probe beneath those desires and get in touch with what we most deeply want *can* literally change our lives. Psalm 37:4 affirms that there are good desires of the heart that God has placed within us. If we are fully in touch with the authentic desire that stirs quietly under the surface chop of our emotional attachments and superficial wanting, we can plot a truer course for our lives rather than being tossed about by every wind of change, every gust of adversity or every whim of cultural expectation.

Have you ever thought about the fact that your desire—for deeper union with God, for love, for belonging, for transformation—is the truest thing about you? We tend to overidentify with external aspects of ourselves such as our giftedness or our woundedness, our personality type, our job or our title, our successes or failures, our identity as husband or wife, mother or father. We think that these aspects of ourselves somehow define us. But in reality, it is our desire for God and our capacity to reach for more of God than we have right now that is the most essential aspect of who we are. Companions in transforming community are increasingly able to see what is truest and most essential in us and call us to it over time. They do this from love and from a deep regard for who they know us to be in God.

For Personal Reflection

How do you respond to the emphasis on the role of desire in the spiritual life? How easy or difficult is it for you to keep your desire open before God?

SOUL SPEAK

There is a place within each one of us that is spiritual in nature. This is the place where God is present to us, and it is often referred to as the soul. In this place God's Spirit witnesses with our spirit to who we really are, and we respond with the intimacy and familiarity of a child calling out to a loving parent (Romans 8:15, 16). The soul is the place where our truest desires make themselves known if we can learn how to listen.

Part of what makes a community spiritually transforming is that it provides a safe zone for getting in touch with our most authentic desires, giving us the opportunity to speak them out loud in the company of those who know how to receive them. Because the group is committed to "listening each other into free speech"—we could even call this "soul speech"!—participants can risk speaking openly and with confidence, knowing that such tender expressions will be received appropriately. The group can then ask clarifying questions that foster reflection on which desires are the most authentic and support us as we discern how we can arrange our lives for what we say we really want.

In Benedictine communities as well as in the early Wesleyan bands of believers (so in both Catholic and Protestant traditions), the operative question for those wanting to join the community was "Do you seek God?" What draws people to such a community

> is reciprocity of desire, God's desire and their desire. Having been touched by God's desire, they want to make their desire for God the determining factor of all of their choices, and they recognize that they need some help to do this. This shared desire gives the group its coherence as well as a shared commitment to be there for one another in that desire. The group's primary task is to make that shared desire explicit and to hold one another in it.[3]

Shared desire to be transformed in and through Christ's presence is the essence of transforming community. It is "the one true thing" for each individual and for the group as it gathers. Over time, as a group comes together to pay attention to their desire for deeper levels of transformation, they learn to ask penetrating questions and support one another in responding faithfully to God's invitations, and they realize they are tapping into the deepest dynamic of the spiritual life. They discover that fresh movements in the spiritual life

begin with the longings that stir way down deep—underneath the noise, the activity, the drivenness of life—and they have a community that helps them pay attention.

The entire life of a good Christian is never less than holy desire.

St. Augustine

OPENING PANDORA'S BOX?

It is not always comfortable to acknowledge our longings. In fact, many of us have developed lives that are full of distraction precisely so we can avoid the discomfort of paying attention to the deeper desires of the heart—those places that feel empty and devoid of what we want or need! Desire also puts us in touch with the places where we have not been able to obtain what we want for ourselves or where we haven't been able to accomplish what's most needed. Our feelings about these aspects of life can range from impotence to hopelessness to rage.

Another reason for the discomfort is that desire can feel a little volatile and out of control, because on some level it is! Only God knows where our honest admissions about desire will take us, and sometimes we will be called upon to own our deeper spiritual desires without knowing what the outcome will be. When Jesus asked blind Bartimaeus, "What do you want me to do for you?" Bartimaeus responded immediately with "My teacher, let me see again" (Mark 10:51). And Jesus healed him right away. This is one possible outcome; at any moment God *can* change, heal, restore—whatever needs to be done. But another outcome for the blind man was that after his healing, the life he had as a beggar no longer fit;

you can't make a living as a beggar when you are healthy and able-bodied! So, the Scriptures tell us, he got up and followed Jesus on the way. After all, where else could he go? What had worked for him in the past no longer worked, so he had to open himself up to the unknown and follow Jesus very closely, letting things unfold without knowing what the outcome would be.

When James and John (and later on their mother) answered Jesus' question about desire by demanding positions of prominence in his kingdom, Jesus followed up with a comment and another question. He replied, "You do not know what you are asking. Are you able to drink the cup that I am about to drink?" (Matthew 20:22), which exposed their lack of understanding about what the coming of God's kingdom was actually going to be like. It also exposed false ambition that was detrimental to the community of disciples, in that it fostered competitiveness and jealousy among them. Who knows what would have happened if these desires had been left to fester in the dark rather than being exposed in the light of Christ's presence?

Mixed motives and unexamined desires lurk within all of us—which is why acknowledging our desire can sometimes feel like opening up Pandora's box. Many of us are afraid to even acknowledge deep desire, given how volatile and out of control it all feels. But make no mistake, *it is even riskier to refuse to acknowledge what is real within us.* Repressed desire only gets stronger and more dangerous the longer we refuse to acknowledge it. How much safer it is for ourselves and everyone around us if we open our desires in Jesus' presence and in the presence of those who know how to accompany us in this place. With the support of such companions, Jesus can help us sift through our desires in a gentle and trustworthy way; we let go of destructive desires so we can embrace what is good and true—for our own good and the good of those around us.

Jesus' compassion for us is in the midst of our desire is real

(Matthew 20:34), and as we walk with Jesus into our own desires, we learn how to be gentle, trustworthy and compassionate companions for each other. We discover that opening up our desire in Christ's presence and in the presence of spiritual companions—even when we're not sure what is true and what is false within us—can foster a new kind of intimacy between us that is oddly satisfying.

Sometimes, as we pay attention to our desire, we are made aware that there are choices for us to make. Jesus' question to the paralyzed man at the pool of Beth-zatha, "Do you want to be made well?" (John 5:6), called for him to take some sort of movement in the direction of his desire. Getting in touch with how badly he wanted healing and his willingness to do what he could catalyzed Jesus' power to do the one thing he could not do for himself. This is at least part of the paradox Paul is referring to when he says that we must work out our own salvation with fear and trembling (Philippians 2:12). He is referring to the fact that there is always God's part and ours on the journey of transformation, which is something we are always discerning.

For Personal Reflection

Take time to review the various biblical stories referred to in this section and sit with the one you are drawn to.

- John 1:35-41: Jesus asks two of John's disciples, "What are you looking for?"
- Matthew 20:20-28: Jesus asks the mother of the sons of Zebedee, "What do you want?"
- Matthew 20:29-34: Jesus asks two blind men, "What do you want me to do for you?" and is moved with compassion.
- Mark 10:36: Jesus asks James and John, the sons of Zebedee, "What is it you want me to do for you?"
- Mark 10:46-52: Jesus asks blind Bartimaeus, "What do you want me to do for you?"

- John 5:2-9: Jesus asks the invalid at the pool of Beth-zatha, "Do you want to be made well?"

Listen for what Jesus has to say to you personally in and through the story you have chosen.

- Am I able to sense Jesus' compassion for the part of me that longs for something I do not yet have? Am I able to feel compassionate for myself?

- Jesus, what do you want to show me about myself as I get more honest about my desires? Which ones seem to come from something false within me, and which ones seem to come from something true?

- Who attempts to silence my desire?

- Do I understand the full ramifications of what I am asking for? What else do I need to know? Am I really ready for what it is I am asking for?

- Is there something Jesus is inviting me to do in order to live into what my heart most wants?

- What aspect of my desire is something only Christ can fulfill or accomplish? What is my part?

RELINQUISHING EACH OTHER TO GOD

"Spirituality concerns what we do with our desire," writes Ronald Rolheiser.[4] The first thing we do with our desire is to get in touch with it and open it up to God, listening for what God has to say to us in the midst of it. We learn to trust that God has plans for us which are deeply good and satisfying, or we wrestle with our lack of trust if we need to. Then, in company with our spiritual companions, we pay attention to the ways God is inviting us to live and make decisions that are consistent with the true desires he has placed within us. We share our desires with our spiritual companions in community so we can support one another in the quest for a life lived in response to these God-given desires.

Becoming a transforming community means we will need to develop a greater capacity to relinquish control to God—control of both our own lives and the lives of others. Rather than desperately trying to fix and manage the outcome of things, we will need to become more and more comfortable allowing God to be God in all of our lives. We will have to learn to wait with each other in that place of not knowing, alert for glimpses of God's guidance and committed to taking courageous action when that guidance is given. We will refrain from trying to fix each other or offering easy, uninsightful responses as we each get in touch with our desires and face into the risky invitations of God in the midst of our desire.

But this is what the community of Jesus is all about. Waiting on Jesus. Together. For each other. As Rose Mary Dougherty writes: "At times the strength of spiritual community lies in the love of people who refrain from getting caught in the trap of trying to fix everything for us, who pray for us and allow us the pain of wilderness, our wants, so that we might become more deeply grounded in God."[5]

ON THE ROAD TOGETHER

As your group gathers again this time, you may choose to practice group spiritual direction as described in the last chapter, but this time you are sharing more specifically about desire and where you are finding yourselves in the biblical stories referenced in the chapter. You can share about the desire that is top-of-mind for you right now—it could have to do with your relationship with God, your desire for personal growth and transformation, family, vocation, physical health and well-being, your desire to make a difference in the world, or anything else.

This time you will add a step in the companioning portion of your time together. As you listen in the silence following each presentation, you may hear a question that would help the presenter clarify their desire, go deeper in their understanding of their desire or consider what that desire might mean for their life. In the companioning that follows the silence, group members may ask open-ended questions—questions they really don't know the answer to—relative to desire.

If they have not connected with a biblical story already, feel free to ask, "In which of the biblical stories referred to in this chapter did you find yourself? As you found yourself in that story, what did Jesus say to you? Which of the questions offered was most penetrating or offered the most insight?"

PRAYING OUR DESIRE

A helpful way to end your time together might be to have someone read Psalm 37:4-7 and then respond as a group with the following prayer.

Oh God, you alone know the depths of each human heart;

GRANT US THE GRACE TO KNOW OUR HEART'S TRUEST DESIRE.
GRANT THAT WE MAY TAKE DELIGHT IN YOU, OH LORD,
TRUSTING YOU WITH ALL OUR HEARTS.
AS WE HOLD OUR DESIRES OPENLY IN YOUR PRESENCE
AND IN EACH OTHER'S PRESENCE,
GRANT US THE COURAGE TO CRY OUT TO YOU;
GRANT US THE FAITH TO BE STILL
AND KNOW THAT YOU ARE GOD,
THAT WE MIGHT WAIT PATIENTLY FOR YOU TO ACT,
IN OUR OWN LIVES AND IN EACH OTHER'S LIVES.

We ask this through Jesus Christ, our Lord.
AMEN.

SOME WOMEN OF OUR GROUP ASTOUNDED US

Men and Women in Community

*Moreover, some women of our group astounded us.
They were at the tomb early this morning, and when they
did not find his body there, they came back and told us
that they had indeed seen a vision of angels
who said that he was alive.*

LUKE 24:22-23

At the risk of stating the obvious, these verses indicate that women
and men together made up the community of Jesus. This might not
seem like a big deal to us, but in the Jewish culture of that day, the
way men and women were together in community around Jesus
was fairly radical. In the synagogues at that time men and women
were separated by a curtain; women and girls were not taught the
Torah, and they served quietly in the background as the menfolk
discussed and argued about spiritual matters. Women were not
allowed to speak or ask questions in public gatherings, let alone
teach or proclaim anything important.

The fact that Jesus appeared first to women at the tomb, interacting with them intimately and substantively about the resurrection, was quite out of the ordinary. He then charged them with
announcing the good news to the rest of the disciples, complete
with instructions for their next steps! That Jesus gave the women
instructions for the male disciples was even more unusual—so
much so that some scholars have suggested this remarkable and
very specific detail serves as historical evidence for the resurrection.
No one trying to fabricate a believable resurrection story would
have included such a culturally unbelievable detail!

What are we to make of this, and who *were* these women?

LAST AT THE CROSS, FIRST AT THE TOMB

The various Gospel accounts all record the fact that women were
the last ones to linger around the cross and the first to arrive at the
tomb where Jesus was buried. They also record the fact that Jesus
appeared to them at the tomb and interacted with them personally
on that resurrection morning, charging them with the responsibility of making the initial proclamation of the good news to the
other disciples.

The names of the women are recorded slightly differently in each account. Matthew 28:1-10 mentions Mary Magdalene and "the other Mary." Mark 16:1-11 identifies Mary Magdalene, Mary the mother of James, and Salome. Initially Luke is somewhat vague, simply indicating that it was "the women" who, having brought spices to anoint Jesus' body, found the stone rolled away and encountered "two men in dazzling clothes." But then later on he makes a point of saying, "Now it was Mary Magdalene, Joanna, Mary the mother of James, and the other women with them who told this to the apostles" (Luke 23:55–24:12). What is consistent in all four of the Gospels is the fact that these ordinary women were part of the transforming community that followed Jesus closely; they were deeply involved with him both in his life and in the pivotal moments surrounding his death, burial and resurrection.

While the rest of the disciples tried to dismiss the women's excited announcement as idle tales (Luke 24:11), Peter found their report convincing enough to at least check on the veracity of their story. And wouldn't you know? The good news these women proclaimed was actually true—making them the first Christian evangelists. (The word *evangelism* literally means "to proclaim the good news.") And they delivered this good news—including instructions for the rest of the disciples about where and how to meet up with Jesus—with all the clarity and conviction that comes from a real encounter with Christ.

BACK TO THE FUTURE

Jesus' presence on the earth brought about many different kinds of needed change in our world, and one of the most significant was a transformation in relationships between men and women. Fresh from God, he was remarkably unencumbered by the cultural norms of the day—norms that had been shaped more by sin patterns in the world than by God's ideal. Even a cursory look at Scripture (especially the Old Testament) reveals disturbing patterns in male-female relationships that were far from God's original and best plan—a partnership model in which man and woman *together* would fully reflect the image of God.

When God brought Eve to Adam as the crowning achievement of his creative efforts, Adam couldn't help exclaiming, "This at last is bone of my bones and flesh of my flesh; this one shall be called Woman, for out of Man this one was taken!" (Genesis 2:23). He recognized her immediately as a kindred spirit, capable of being the partner and companion God knew he needed. There didn't seem to be any indication of hierarchy, just a sense of fulfillment in finally having "a helper as his partner."[1] They stood shoulder to shoulder and received their instructions to share the responsibility for being fruitful and multiplying, filling the earth, subduing it and ruling together over all living things (Genesis 1:28-29). When God took a step back and surveyed his final creative effort—male and female made in his image—for the first time in the entire creation process he commented that it was "*very* good" (1:31). Today we would call this the complete package!

Fairly quickly, however, a problem developed in the perfect world God had created. In addition to the clear mandate to be fruitful and multiply and share dominion over the earth, God had also given specific instructions to Adam (before Eve was created) that they were not to eat of one particular tree that God clearly identified. Both Adam and Eve knew of this instruction, and each in their own way chose to disobey God, causing dire consequences for the human race. The fallout from this one event included the introduction of sin and guilt, shame and blame, wrongful domination and seduction into male-female relationships. This was in direct contradiction to the oneness, equality and mutuality that characterized God's best plan for gender relations—which he established in creation and reclaimed through the redeeming work of Christ as Paul summarizes it in Galatians 3:28.

In Genesis 3:14-19, God predicts specific ways in which human beings would experience brokenness and pain in various aspects of their existence. There would be particular enmity between Satan and the woman. Women would long for loving relationships with men but would experience wrongful domination instead, and the fruit of their intimacy would be pain in childbearing. Men would experience work to be backbreaking and frustrating as they coaxed the ground to yield its fruit through blood, sweat and tears.

All of these *predictions* about the various consequences of sin did indeed come true, but it was certainly not God's *prescription* for how things should be. In fact, contained within God's prediction was a promise that there would be One who would come and bring redemption to all facets of human sin and brokenness—including the sin and brokenness between men and women. That One has come, and his name is Jesus. And his presence immediately disrupted sinful patterns in gender relations, initiating new ones that more accurately reflected God's heart toward women and men in his community.

BEYOND THE CURSE

Every time Jesus interacted with women or helped men and women interact with one another, he modeled new relating patterns that began the process of redeeming all of us from the oppressive effects of the curse on male-female relationships. That is why we see Jesus talking to an immoral woman about theology, worship, the state of her relationships and the state of her soul (John 4). It's why we see him pointing out to a group of religious leaders that a woman caught in adultery was no more guilty than they were (John 8:1-11), and why we see him receiving Mary's act of worship as much more meaningful than anything that was going on in the synagogues (John 12:1-8). It's why some of his best friends were women—indicated by his visits in their homes (Luke 10:38-42), the give-and-take in their conversations (John 11:1-44), and the fact that they were last at the cross and first at the tomb (Mark 15:40-47).

Every interaction Jesus had with those who followed him closely did something to shift the balance and the tone of relationships between men and women among those closest to him. In this very real and tangible way, Christ did redeem us from the curse of the law (Galatians 3:13). It is not surprising, then, that after Jesus' death things were just plain different. When the disciples returned to Jerusalem to await the Holy Spirit, they were all together in the upper room, and "all these were constantly devoting themselves to prayer, together with certain women, including Mary the mother of Jesus" (Acts 1:14). Again, in Jewish cultural practice it was unheard of that men and women would be together in such an intimate way, but by now these new Christ-followers were more influenced by Jesus than by the surrounding culture! On the day of Pentecost they were still together as tongues of fire rested on each one of them and they were filled with the Holy Spirit and were speaking in tongues (Acts 2:4).

> The wounds inflicted by men and women on each other constitute the fundamental fault line running beneath all other human conflict.... It is the biggest reconciliation issue of all, outside of our need to be reconciled to God the Father.
>
> John Dawson

When Peter got up to preach and explain these events to those who were watching, he pointed out that this was a fulfillment of Joel's prophecy that when God poured forth his Spirit it would be for everyone. Sons and daughters, men and women would prophesy—that is to say, speak forth the mind of God (Acts 2:16-18). And they did! As the early church grew, women worked right alongside men in spreading the gospel and planting churches. In some cases it was women (such as Lydia in Philippi) who were prime movers in getting churches started by hosting them in their homes. Other women taught theology (Priscilla), served as ministers or deacons (Phoebe), prophesied (Philip's daughters) and simply worked very hard (see Romans 16:1-16).

First Corinthians 12 put into words what was already in evidence in the early church: to each one is given the manifestation of the Spirit (spiritual gift) without regard to gender. This was entirely consistent with Peter's assertion "that God shows no partiality" (Acts 10:34) and that we are all members of a "royal priesthood," charged with proclaiming "the mighty acts of him who called you out of darkness into his marvelous light" (1 Peter 2:9-10).

When Paul described the oneness and mutuality of the body of Christ in 1 Corinthians 12 and Ephesians 4, it was much more than just a theory—it was the way the men and women who were Jesus' earliest followers were already working together and had worked together from the very beginning. Paul summed up the impact of Jesus' redeeming presence in the new community this way: "In Christ Jesus you are all children of God through faith. As many of you as were baptized into Christ have clothed yourself with Christ. There is no longer Jew or Greek, there is no longer slave or free, there is no longer male and female; for all of you are one in Christ Jesus" (Galatians 3:26-28). Rather than experiencing these physical characteristics as cause for limitation and discrimination, in the body of Christ we experience something wholly different from what the effects of sin produced.

All of this is to say that *oneness, equality and mutuality across lines of race, socioeconomic status and gender are significant aspects of transforming community.* In communities gathered around the transforming presence of Jesus, women and men of different races, ethnic groupings and income levels experience—perhaps for the first time—equal opportunities and invitations to serve, lead and participate in the life of the community. Everywhere you look you see men and women with their sleeves rolled up serving side by side, in their clerical robes preaching and leading worship side by side, or in the board room discerning side by side. Since men and women together fully reflect the image of God, how could it be any other way in the community that he has formed through the person and work of Christ?

For Personal Reflection

What have you observed about relationships between women and men in the body of Christ? Have you witnessed and experienced the kind of equality and mutuality described here? How do you respond to the vision of relationships between brothers and sisters in Christ described here?

PRACTICING ONENESS

The change Jesus' presence wrought in male-female relationships is one of the most striking elements of the transforming community that gathered around Jesus. Many churches and ministry communities today are still in the process of discovering what the oneness he taught and modeled really looks like—especially across lines of gender.

Paul uses the metaphor of the family to characterize our relationship to one another in the community of Jesus. He speaks of us as the family of God and men and women as brothers and sisters in that family. I find this particularly inspiring because I have two brothers with whom I am very close. This metaphor speaks to me deeply about the love and intimacy, equality and mutuality that is possible in relationships between men and women in the body of Christ. If there was any hint of hierarchy imposed upon these relationships due to gender, or any hint of dominance or misuse of sexuality, real relationships between us would be untenable. In fact, it is the absence of such issues, along with the intentional cultivation of spiritual friendship and collegiality, that makes these relationships the great blessing God intends them to be.

Because of our love and care for each other, there are no "men's issues" or "women's issues" that need to be handled in segregated groups; there are just human issues that we care about together because they affect us all—in our family and beyond. Our interest in and care for one another extends to all areas of life: our spouses, marriages and children, our vocational lives, providing for our families, our spiritual growth and discipleship, our attempts at wholeness in our family of origin, joys and struggles related to sexuality and fidelity, and our thoughts and opinions about a wide variety of issues facing our world today. Over the years we have grown in learning how to share equally in the work of family life (initiating and planning family events, cooking, hosting, caring for children, working through relational issues, etc.) based on gifts and interests rather than gender stereotypes. And we make it a priority to share hobbies, interests and fun together, as much as we are able given our geographical distance from one another.

It is hard to imagine that these relationships could be healthy without this kind of mutuality, equality and shared responsibility. This is what I think of when I envision what is possible between brothers and sisters in the family of God. Reflecting on Jesus' relationship with women and our experiences in our own human families inspires us to consider what it might look *for us* to cultivate transforming communities of women and men who are discovering what it means to be brothers and sisters in the family of God. In such communities, our participation would be shaped not by gender stereotypes and limitations but by our shared faith in the One who redeems us all, our shared baptism through which we have been raised to new life in Christ, and the shared Spirit who bestows spiritual gifts upon us all for the building up of the body of Christ without regard to race, gender or socioeconomic status. In such communities, our relationships are grounded in brotherly and sisterly love rather than keeping our distance from one another due to sexual fears and temptations or the magnification of differences that cause us to feel we are completely "other" than one another.

For Personal Reflection

Think about your relationships with your brothers (if you are a woman) or your sisters (if you are a man). What were those relationships like? Did you and do you experience them as relationships of equality, mutual influence and love, or something else? Are these experiences the same as or different from what you experience with members of the other gender in the body of Christ?

INCLUDING ONE ANOTHER

There are very concrete ways we can open to the transforming presence of Christ in all our relationships, particularly our relationships with brothers and sisters in Christ. First of all, we can be more intentional about including one another and perhaps even pay more attention to the ways in which we subtly exclude or diminish one another. One of the defining characteristics of the

New Testament church was a radical kind of inclusivity, starting with the issue of race. God went to great lengths to teach the Christ-followers to affirm the conversion experiences of the Gentiles and welcome them based on evidence of the Holy Spirit in their lives rather than insisting they be circumcised. This was their first challenge related to including those who had previously been excluded or limited due to some physical characteristics; their mandate was to welcome people based on the condition of their heart in relation to God, not on physical characteristics. Peter expressed it this way in relation to his experience with Cornelius: "The Spirit told me . . . not to make a distinction between them and us. . . . If then God gave them the same gift that he gave us when we believed in the Lord Jesus Christ, who was I that I could hinder God?" (Acts 11:12, 17).

What was so remarkable about this new development was the fact that circumcision was one of the most sacred cows among the Jewish people: it was a symbol of their status as God's chosen people, instituted by God himself. Now God was challenging something God himself had put in place because it no longer served his larger purpose—the redemption of the whole world. It took attentiveness and responsiveness to God *in the moment* to recognize this and live into it.

As a culture we are at the point where we at least give mental assent to the fact that people of all races and classes are equal in God's sight; however, many are still in the process of making the final application to gender as well. Since Paul himself connects the dots between the issue of race, socioeconomic status and gender in Galatians 3:28, we, too, must learn what it means to include and welcome one another's true selves and gifts regardless of gender, as each one's gifts and interests are given by God and breathed into life through his Spirit.

While we still wrestle at times with the tendency to subtly exclude others or make assumptions about them on the basis of race, in most circles today there is at least a basic agreement that racial stereotyping and the resulting discrimination are not at all consistent with our Christian ideals and commitments. And yet, it is easy to fall into the same kind of stereotyping and exclusion when it comes to men and women; some Christian communities today still hold to a theological position that prevents women from being free to serve God in all the ways he has called and gifted them, which greatly hampers the sharing of life together in Christ.

When these two elements (gender stereotyping and theological perspectives that limit women) are combined, small groups and whole congregations can fall into a pattern where women serve refreshments and take care of the children while the men preach and lead—or where women are limited in the ways they can serve while men are free to exercise their gifts unencumbered by limits due to gender. It may be that women and men are routinely segregated into separate ministries based on an assumption that there are certain topics just men talk about or just women talk about—or women's spirituality and men's spirituality are framed as being so fundamentally different that it is not useful for men and women to be together and talk openly about a full range of human experience.

To counter this tendency, we can seek a dynamic mix of women and men teaching and leading, cooking and preparing refreshments, taking care of children and exercising their spiritual gifts in the community, in small groups and in the community as a whole. We can invite each person to share about their spiritual gifts, personal hobbies and interests—even those that go against gender stereotypes—and brainstorm how those gifts can be offered within the group. There may be women in the group who are strong teachers and men who love to cook or care for children and vice versa, which make things a lot more interesting! We can mix it up and have couples or different combinations of men and women combine their gifts to offer different aspects of what's needed, rather than relegating certain tasks to one gender or another. Perhaps we, too, will then be able to say, "The women of our group astounded us . . . and the men, too!"

LISTENING WITH ATTENTION

Closely connected with including one another is the commitment to *listen to one other with love, respect and genuine interest.* We have already reflected on listening in general, but it may take another level of commitment to listen to one another across lines of gender, believing that we all share the same basic experience of being human. Women and men have much to offer one another in community if we are willing to listen and be influenced by one another, rather than dismissing each other. In worshiping communities I was part of during childhood and young adulthood, women were not allowed to speak in worship services or public forums. This simple pattern communicated powerfully that men were more worthy of being listened to than women. In many churches today, women still do not have the freedom to speak from the pulpit or to provide leadership as pastors or elders. This communicates subtly that women are not to be heard and listened to with the same kind of influence and authority as men.

By the same token, when men and women are segregated too much in separate small groups and ministries, the subtle message can be that we don't need each other—that men don't need to hear from women regarding the issues they face or that women don't need a perspective from men on the issues they face. Or that there are certain aspects of the human experience that women care about more than men and vice versa. In transforming community, there is a deep-seated belief that none of us have the right to say to another, "I have no need of you"—on the basis of gender or any other characteristic. Transforming community is a context in which women and men can approach one another with curiosity and a genuine sense of anticipation regarding how we might speak into, listen to and influence one another's lives.

Recently I preached all four services in a mainline church that was part of a denomination that has ordained women for years. I assumed that having a woman in the pulpit was rather routine for this congregation, so I didn't think much of it; however, at the end of one service as I stood in the sanctuary to greet people, a woman approached holding the hand of a little girl who must have been about eight years old. With tears in her eyes, she told me that this was the first time she had seen a woman in that pulpit and the first time she had heard a woman preach! Profuse in her gratitude, she kept looking from my face into the face of her little girl, who was looking up at me with what appeared to be awe. And I could tell that part of this mother's emotion was her deep desire for her little girl to see that God can and does speak through women to his church—the body of Christ—and that all options for serving God are open to her.

On the one hand, my heart was broken that there are still places in this world where the voices of men and women are not heard together in harmony proclaiming the good news of Jesus. On the other hand, I was grateful to be part of a sacred moment in which a little girl could have a more complete vision of what life in the body of Christ—and what her life—can be like.

HONORING SEXUALITY IN COMMUNITY

In order to experience transforming community, we must acknowledge, with eyes wide open, the sexual dynamic that is present between men and women when we are together and commit ourselves to *respect and honor the power of sexuality.* In a secular culture where sexuality is overplayed and often abused and a religious culture where sexuality is often repressed and avoided, transforming community can be a place where the gift of our sexuality is acknowledged and received while, at the same time, its power is respected and handled wisely.

All of us have experienced moments where someone else's infidelity or our own sexual urges bring up fears that can be pretty overwhelming. At the same time we long for a community where we can be held safely as the human selves we are, experiencing the fullness and the goodness God intended for us as men and women in relationship with each other. In transforming community we learn to experience and even enjoy the good chemistry that is produced when male and female—the core elements of the human race—get together. It is possible for the sparks generated by male and female in close proximity to be harnessed toward building a fire that can warm us all rather than being allowed to fly out of control and burn down the whole forest. Tending the sparks wisely so they don't start a forest fire will involve

- facing our fears and moving beyond them so we don't remain victims of sin and cultural pathologies;

- establishing good and healthy connections between our sexuality and our spirituality as beings created in God's image;

- cultivating self-awareness and taking responsibility for any transformation needed regarding any distortions within our experience of sexuality;

- opening our sexual longings to God and learning how to seek his care and wisdom regarding how such legitimate longings can be met;

- moving toward each other in Christlike expressions of love, friendship and partnership;

- (if married) cultivating marriages that are healthy, satisfying and honest; (if single) being intentional about expressing sexuality in healthy ways.

What a worthy goal it would be for men and women in transforming community to model relationships that are closer to God's ideal and Jesus' example than the cultural distortions for which we have often settled! And what a testimony such a community would be to a world lost in a sea of confusion, selfishness and sin—sometimes because it has never been winsomely presented with another way.[2]

Certainly there is a fine line between respecting the power of sexuality and refusing to live out of our fears, but it is the line that Jesus himself walked. The willingness to move beyond fear and paranoia to real brotherly and sisterly love in Christ is completely contrary to what we see in our secular hook-up culture and also in much of our repressed religious subculture. Celia Allison Hahn calls this "sexual paradox," which she identifies as

> a call for women and men to live faithfully in the tension of two realities: awareness of our feelings and drives and also the call to behave in responsible ways. Sexual paradox invites us to live where the currents of energy spark back and forth. People discover new sources of vitality when they hold opposites together in tension. And there is a lot of good energy in male-female collaboration—energy that is one of the most precious gifts of God for the people of God.[3]

———————— ON THE ROAD TOGETHER ————————

Share with one another how your early experiences in church and culture, in your family, and with your brothers and sisters has shaped your understanding of what is possible in relationships between men and women in Christian community today.

Take time to discuss the Scriptures referenced in this chapter—those describing God's created ideal for male-female relationships as well as Jesus' actions and behaviors toward women and men in his own close community. Which scriptural insights are you drawn to as you reflect on how women and men can be together in transforming community?

Where do you find affirmation for how you are currently approaching relationships between men and women in community, and where do you feel challenged?

How might your community practice the kind of mutuality and oneness observed in these Scriptures and in this chapter? Be specific about what that might look like for your group.

A Prayer Affirming Our Life Together as Brothers and Sisters in Christ

Leader: As a community gathered in the transforming
              presence of Jesus,

ALL: WE AFFIRM
              THAT, AS MEN AND WOMEN, WE ARE MADE IN
              GOD'S IMAGE,
              BEFRIENDED BY CHRIST, EMPOWERED BY THE
              SPIRIT.

Leader: With God's people everywhere,

ALL: WE AFFIRM
GOD'S GOODNESS AT THE HEART OF CREATION
PLANTED MORE DEEPLY THAN ALL THAT IS
WRONG.

Leader: With all creation,

ALL: WE CELEBRATE
THE MIRACLE AND WONDER OF LIFE;
AND THE UNFOLDING PURPOSES OF GOD,
FOREVER AT WORK IN OURSELVES AND THE
WORLD.

Leader: Move among us, O God; give us life:

ALL: LET YOUR PEOPLE REJOICE IN YOU.

Leader: As brothers and sisters in your family,

ALL: MAKE OUR HEARTS CLEAN WITHIN US:
RENEW US IN MIND AND SPIRIT.

Leader: Give us the joy of your help, O God;

ALL: WITH YOUR SPIRIT OF FREEDOM SUSTAIN US.
AMEN.[4]

WAS IT NOT NECESSARY THAT THE MESSIAH SHOULD SUFFER?

The Nature of the Spiritual Journey

*Then he said to them, "Oh, how foolish you are, and how
slow of heart to believe all that the prophets have declared!
Was it not necessary that the Messiah should suffer
these things and then enter into his glory?"*

LUKE 24:25-26

If you ask people to name a time in their spiritual life when they grew the most or felt closest to God, many people will refer to a time when they had to endure pain, loss or suffering. Even though whatever they endured was real and they probably would not choose to go back, looking at that experience through the lens of what God was doing through it offers a whole different perspective. In fact, sometimes what they feel they gained was so valuable that they might even say, "Even though it was hard, I wouldn't trade it for anything."

This is exactly what Jesus did for the two disciples on the Emmaus Road—he gave the gift of helping them see what they had been through from a whole different perspective. Having listened to them so well, he had now earned the right to speak. And when he did speak, he offered them so much more than platitudes or mere comfort regarding the troubles they had seen. He offered them a completely different set of lenses through which to view their recent traumatic experiences. The first lens Jesus offered (and the subject of this chapter) was to draw attention to the nature of the spiritual journey—the paschal rhythm of death, burial and resurrection as the essential rhythm of the spiritual life, and of suffering as a necessary part of it. With so few words Jesus captured the essence of the spiritual journey: "Was it not necessary that the Messiah should suffer these things and then enter into his glory?"

He had, of course, tried to describe this aspect of the spiritual life earlier on while he was still with his disciples, but it was impossible for them to grasp it until they were experiencing it for themselves. Matthew 16 records the fact that Jesus told his disciples in great detail that he "must go to Jerusalem and undergo great suffering" and eventually be killed, but Peter in particular just would not have it. He actually rebuked Jesus, saying, "God forbid it, Lord! This must never happen to you." And Jesus said to him, "Get behind me, Satan! You are a stumbling block to me; for you are setting your mind not on divine things but on human things" (Matthew 16:21-23).

THE GIFT THAT KEEPS ON GIVING

Peter's (and presumably the other dis-ciples') difficulty accepting the fact that Jesus would have to suffer raises a so-bering possibility for spiritual com-panions to consider, and it is this: in our

> *Resurrection is when one moment reveals the meaning of all moments.*
>
> Richard Rohr

attempts to be loyal and faithful and helpful (as Peter was surely trying to be), we too could be a distraction and even a stumbling block to one another if we fail to understand the nature of the spiritual journey and God's divine purposes in all aspects of the journey, including suffering. How confusing it can be if members of a spiritual community have fundamentally different ideas about what the spiritual journey is all about.

For instance, if one's vision of the journey is shaped by a "success gospel" in which the sign of God's blessing is that everything is always "up and to the right" while others understand it to be a series of "necessary deaths" in which we let go of that which is false so what is truest within us can fully emerge, we could actually do more harm than good in our attempts to companion one another! If some in the group believe that growth in the spiritual life is marked by increasing certitude while others are being drawn into the kinds of questions that defy easy answers and trite sayings, we could actually thwart what God is trying to do in their lives.

One of the most valuable offerings we can make to one another in transforming community is the perspective that enables us to "see through" to what is really going on spiritually speaking, no matter how painful the events and experiences might be. To affirm that God is at work even in our suffering can be redemptive if we allow it to be.

The Heart of the Matter

What Jesus did here in so few words was to draw attention to the heart of the Christian story. To those who had experienced the weekend's traumatizing events, he was pointing out that they were not merely witnesses to a terrible injustice; they were actually witnessing the great saving act of God accomplished in and through Jesus' suffering and the sacrifice of his life.

In theory, this would have been a concept the disciples were familiar with, since they were in fact Jews. The word *paschal* comes from the Hebrew *pesach*, or "passover," alluding to the story of the exodus, in which the blood of an unblemished lamb marking the doorposts of the Israelites' homes prompted the angel of death to pass over them as it moved through the land of Egypt. The firstborn sons of those who placed their trust in God by keeping his instruction lived, but the firstborn of those who did not died. The ability to trust God for their very lives—symbolized by this action—became such a defining characteristic of the Jewish people that they reenact it and celebrate it annually to this day. As important as the first Passover was in Jewish history, it was also a foreshadowing of the coming of Christ, who is our perfect, unblemished Passover Lamb. In the same way that the blood of the Passover lamb protected Israelite households from certain death, Jesus' blood covers us, protects us and brings about our salvation. And in his death he modeled for us the laying down of that which is temporal in order to gain that which is eternal.

This necessary rhythm of suffering and death, burial and resurrection was the *spiritual* reality Jesus' disciples were living through in a condensed fashion as they experienced the events of that first "Good" Friday, waited numbly through that first Holy Saturday and tried to find their way back home on that first Resurrection Sunday.

Even though they hadn't been able to make sense of it yet, Jesus' journey from death to life was revealing the true nature of the spiritual life. And as he interpreted the events of the previous days, he was signaling to them that we too must "die" if we desire to be raised to new life in Christ. We, too, must lay down *anything* that is a hindrance to us spiritually, so we can walk in newness of life.

To be clear, Jesus was perfect, so there was no sin in him that needed to die; but he did need to "let go" of the physical body that limited him to being in one place at a time, here and not there, earthbound rather than seated on the right hand of God in the heavenly places. The relinquishment of his physical body in death freed him for even greater presence through the coming of the Holy Spirit. That is why he could say to his disciples that it was actually *to their advantage* that he went away physically (John 16:7)—so that he could be present to them in a new and unencumbered way. The difference in Jesus' journey and our own is that most often what needs to die in us are the sins, negative patterns and false-self attachments that limit the freedom of our true-self-in-God. This letting go feels like suffering and death because on some level it is; but what we need to know is that it is death unto life.

OUT WITH THE OLD AND IN WITH THE NEW

All this talk of death and suffering might seem like a rather dour—if not harsh!—view of the spiritual life, but I assure you it is not. The only thing we stand to lose in this process of death and dying is that which is not needed anyway. In fact, what needs to die is not really even real; it is the set of illusions that is the false self. The true self—our very essence—is hidden with Christ in God and is waiting to be revealed (Colossians 3:1-3). There is a kind of freedom on the other side that we can only imagine. As David Benner points out, the true-self-in-Christ is who, in reality, you are and who you are becoming. It is not something you need to construct through a process of self-improvement or deconstruct by means of psychological analysis. It is not an object to be grasped. Rather, it is your total self as you were created by God and as you are being redeemed in Christ. It is the image of God that you are—the unique face of God that has been set aside from eternity for you.[1]

And lest we turn this into an occasion for narcissistic navel-gazing or human effort and striving, Benner quickly adds, "We do not find our true self by seeking it. Rather, we find it by seeking God."[2]

This truth about the nature of the spiritual journey can be powerfully disorienting and reorienting for transforming communities as we affirm that the most profound experience of the road between the now and the not yet is the one between the "now" of who we know ourselves to be currently and the "not yet" of who we are becoming. Beyond our initial conversion experience, there is an ongoing call to conversion that leads us step by step to an increasing ability to live freely as we were meant to live in God. Through his life and through his death, Jesus taught us that we must lose our life (small l) in order to gain that which is Life indeed (capital L).

Father Thomas Keating writes, "The spiritual journey is not a career or a success story. It is a series of small humiliations of the false self that become more and more profound. These make room inside us for the Holy Spirit to come and heal. What prevents us from being available to God is gradually evacuated [as] we keep getting closer and closer to our Center"[3]—the place where God dwells within us as redeemed people. Oftentimes it is suffering that initiates the necessary "evacuations"; even Jesus learned obedience through the things he suffered (Hebrews 5:8).

> ### *For Personal Reflection*
>
> Stop for a bit and ponder the nature of the spiritual journey as a journey from the false self to the true-self-in-Christ—and your willingness to be on *that* journey. Let yourself see and know and feel this hidden and most personal experience of living between the "now and the not yet" along with your longing for the more that God knows you to be. As you ponder, lean into the hope that your true self really does exist—hidden with Christ in God, held in trust for you as you let go of the old and welcome the new! If a prayer emerges, you may want to speak out loud to God or write your prayer in your journal.

THE JOURNEY FROM DEATH TO LIFE

The goal of the Christian journey is surrender—the ability to trust God with our whole selves and our very lives—rather than relying on attempts to achieve safety and security, affection and approval, power and control for ourselves on our own terms. It is an increasing capacity to be given over to the love and the will of God in radical trust, just as Jesus was. Beyond potlucks and pastoral care, *this* is the real journey that spiritual companions embark on together, and it can be a harrowing one.

Our own Christian tradition provides a road map for the journey between the "now" of living primarily out of false-self patterns and the "not yet" of living as our true-self-in-God. The classic model of the spiritual journey identifies four stages in the Christian journey: awakening, purgation, illumination and union. Robert Mulholland summarizes these masterfully in his book *Invitation to a Journey*, and he points out that these stages can function on two levels: they can encompass the entire journey of salvation that begins with awakening to God and culminates in complete union with God in the life to come, *and* they can be seen as the path we experience in a particular area where we have been stuck in unlikeness to Christ. It is possible to be at one stage of the journey in one area of our life while being at a different stage in another, but what is consistent is that often it is some kind of suffering that gets the ball rolling and starts the process.

For instance, while awakening could be God's call to conversion in general (prior to salvation), it can also be a call to conversion regarding *a particular area* of our unlikeness to Christ. Suffering often initiates this kind of awakening, as we see more clearly our reliance on and our attachment to that which is not God. Awakening leads to purgation, in which God strips us of whatever it is that is preventing us from relying solely on him and moves us to increasing relinquishment of whatever it is we have been clinging to. While this can feel quite painful and out of our control, the one choice we do have is whether we will keep resisting, fighting and giving in to cynicism or will surrender and cooperate with God's work in us. This is the part that feels most like death—the grain of wheat falling into the ground so it can bring forth much fruit.

Richard Rohr comments on the necessity of this kind of surrender when he writes,

> I don't think we can chart its course ahead of time. Our own private salvation projects seldom do the job. Surrender is something that is done to us, more than something we do ourselves. Someone else must determine the timing, the circumstances, the shape of the ordeal. None of us can engineer our own transformation—or it would not be transformation at all but merely cosmetic surgery to make us think well of ourselves. You can't choose ahead of time which dragon you'll slay or how you will slay it. It will probably slay you—so just be sure you are well-practiced in dying.[4]

The good news is that after this necessary suffering, the next stage is illumination, in which we start to recognize the fruit of that suffering—greater freedom for God and greater intimacy with God as he leads us into new ways of being and doing in the world.

This necessary suffering leads to new life as the authentic self that God created, that God knows so intimately and that God invites to live free and unencumbered in his presence. We emerge from this experience able to walk in newness of life and union with God in the place where we had been resisting. We experience a more complete surrender as we "become Christ" and his nature is lived freely in and through us at that point where previously we were unlike him and trusting in ourselves (2 Peter 1:3, 4).

This is the married couple who have been through an infidelity, and having stayed with one another and allowed their illusion of the perfect marriage to fall away, they discover more honest selves and truer intimacy on the other side. There is something about them now that is so much more real as the light of God shines through them as earthen and earthy vessels.

This is the man whose wife has left him, and he must accept an unwanted divorce. As he struggles to accept the death of his dream of what his life would be, he quietly speaks of a newfound intimacy with God that never would have been possible while he was clinging to an ideal that didn't exist.

This is the woman who loses a job she had allowed to define her; in the aftermath she realizes she never could have discovered her overidentification with her work until it was gone. Now she moves with freedom and ease because what she suffered created space for her to find her truest identity in God. Now she knows that nothing she does externally will affect her basic identity.

This is the mother and father who oriented their whole lives around their hope that their children would turn out a certain way, and when a child makes heartbreaking mistakes and squanders opportunity, they are able to let go and trust God—finally—with what is most precious to them. Even though they care deeply for their child, they also know that whatever happens, they will be okay in God.

This is the person who discovers he has cancer, and after denying and being angry and arguing with God, he is finally able to let go of willfulness and allow God to be in control of his destiny.

Was it not necessary for the Messiah and for us to "suffer all these things" in order to enter into the "glory" of being with God in some new and more complete way? Yes. Would we wish suffering on ourselves or anyone else? No. Do we grieve whatever losses there might have been? Yes, of course we do. But are we walking around now as resurrected people because we have lost our life in order to find it? You'd better believe it!

PERSPECTIVES ON THE JOURNEY

I remember a conversation I had with a young pastor and several of his elders while leading a retreat a number of years ago. I had just given a talk on the place in the spiritual journey where God begins to dismantle those things that have seemed so certain and so very sturdy in our lives—our sense of ourselves and how we identify ourselves to others, our thoughts about who God is and how God can be found, our reliance on our preferred patterns of thinking and functioning as a way of keeping ourselves safe in the world, and so on. I explained that this season of the spiritual journey can feel like a kind of death because something really is dying—the false self is falling away so that the true-self-in-God can emerge more fully. And since the false self is the only self we know at this point, it feels like we are losing everything when what is really happening is that we are losing our life (lowercase) so we can attain to that which is Life indeed.

I thought I had done a fairly good job of explaining all of this until we were walking to lunch and this young pastor asked, "Does everybody have to go through the kind of death you just described? If so, is there any way we can 'bring it on' a little quicker so we get to the other side of it?" His sincerity in asking the question was so sweet that I wished I could have spared him the answer, but all I could think to say was "Well, if even Jesus had to die in order for the will of God to come forth, then it's pretty certain that we will have to die as well." It was the truest thing I knew how to say—perhaps not exactly what he wanted to hear, but true nonetheless. And that truth, offered at the right moment, is the truth we really need.

—————— ON THE ROAD TOGETHER ——————

After reflecting on this chapter personally, share with each other which stage of the spiritual journey you feel you are in. You could share where you are in general, or you could choose a specific aspect of your journey toward Christlikeness and share where you are experiencing yourself to be on that journey and what continues to propel you forward.

How does Jesus' rhythm of death, burial and resurrection, along with the explanation of the stages of the spiritual journey, offer you a perspective on your own spiritual life? What guidance does it offer? What hope or encouragement?

If it feels appropriate, you might want to share with your group how they can support you at this stage in your journey of transformation. Members of the group should be careful not to fix, problem solve or give advice to one another. Instead, listen carefully to how each person would like to be companioned, and explore how you might offer what they have requested.

Fall Garden

In fall
the garden is spent
having given its all.

Cucumber vines lie exhausted on the ground.
Tomato plants list to one side.
Cornstalks stand dignified and empty.
Sunflower faces droop earthward,
shades of their former selves.

All that has not been claimed lies moldering in the dirt—
*   a bruised tomato, a forsaken pepper . . .*
*   a misshapen pumpkin, a trampled stalk of beans.*
What came from the earth is returning
to the place from whence it came.

There is intimacy here,
*   in the fall garden,*
*   gazing at living things in their demise.*
I want to avert my eyes, avoid this tender grief.
Is this life or is this death? I cannot tell.

Ah, but there is a beauty here
*   amid all this death and dying.*
To have given one's self fully
at least once:
that is the thing.

To have spent oneself in an explosion of color,
*   to have offered one's body for food,*
*   one's very soul for nourishment . . .*
It is an unseemly generosity,
beauty of another kind.

In fall
the garden says, "This is my life, given for you."
And we are fed.

Ruth Haley Barton

HE EXPLAINED
THE SCRIPTURES TO THEM

Finding Our Story in His Story

*Then beginning with Moses and all the prophets,
he interpreted to them the things about
himself in all the scriptures.*

LUKE 24:27

One of the most meaningful community experiences I can remember came through the spiritual guidance of my good friend and ministry colleague Adele Calhoun. We were on retreat with a group of leaders who were gathering for the first time to be more intentional about our spiritual transformation so we could discern God's will among us. Each of us came prepared to lead one session of the retreat in the way we felt led. Adele chose to lead our group in an exercise she called "Finding Ourselves in the Story." She introduced the exercise by explaining that each of us is a part of the larger story God is writing. "We are all chapters in God's book," she said. "We are a word of God, too."

She went on to say that finding our place in the context of the larger redemption story is an important point of integration as we find ourselves named, revealed and known in the pages of Scripture. We discover that God authors the biblical story—the written record of his ongoing presence and action in the world— and he authors the story of our lives as well. The exercise was simply this: as we entered into a time of solitude we were to reflect on this set of questions:

> Where is the place in Scripture where you find yourself exclaiming, "My story is being told here!"? Where among the biblical characters have you found yourself named, understood and received? What are the events and life circumstances that have shaped you most profoundly, and how does finding that part of your own story in His-story foster a reverent awareness that God is authoring your life?

We were not to make this an intellectual exercise where we went rifling through our Bibles in search of someone to admire. Nor was it an exercise of the ego in which we set our sights on someone we aspired to be like. Rather, it was a spiritual exercise in which we were to invite God to show us our place in the story—in God's time and in God's way. There was to be no grasping and clinging—just openness to what God wanted to show us, asking that our eyes would be opened to see our lives in new ways as we pondered this question throughout the afternoon.

MEANING IN THE MADNESS

After dinner that evening, our group gathered around a roaring fire to share with each other where we found ourselves in the story. A time of silence helped us transition from the joviality of the dinner hour to a quieter listening posture as we realized we were crossing over onto holy ground. The first person to share described himself as Lazarus; he had felt spiritually dead for a long time but now had a sense he was emerging from the tomb, ready to be unwrapped from his grave clothes. Another found herself in the story of Moses, whose experience of being an alien in a foreign land corresponded with her experience as a missionary kid and always feeling like an outsider. There was Mary, who had been incubating and was now birthing something new and was experiencing the rawness, vulnerability and misunderstanding that can accompany such birth.

There was Jonathan, who was looking for his David—a leader worthy of his followership—after having experienced several disappointments with the failures of leaders he had tried to follow. Another identified with Barnabas and was grappling with the reality that he was more of a behind-the-scenes encourager than an up-front leader. A devout Catholic among us identified himself as Peter, longing for unity in the body of Christ. In particular, he shared his pain regarding the rift between Protestants and Catholics and how his own sense of calling resonated with Jesus' statement that Peter would be the rock on which he would build his church. And on it went—each story more tender than the last.

What was so profound about this experience was how real it was, and how deep was our sharing. Even though we had already introduced ourselves to each other by sharing basic information (where we were from, what our vocational context was, our family status), this conversation left us feeling like we knew each other in a much more essential way. We were strangely encouraged as we allowed the stories of these biblical characters to affect how we understood and assigned meaning to our own life experiences—no matter how blessed or how difficult they had been. As we realized that even the most personal aspects of our own stories could be found in the pages of Scripture, they started to make more sense. Looked at through the lens of God's purposes, our life experiences could be interpreted quite differently.

In the company of others, this new way of seeing yielded fresh understanding about circumstances and events that had, up to this point, made very little sense at all. We found ourselves drawn deeper into fellowship with the small of group of us who were gathered around that fire together, yes, but also deeper into the communion of saints, apostles and martyrs who had gone before us. Each of us experienced ourselves to be one of many as we got to know our "family" and discovered family resemblances and shared experiences that we had not been as aware of previously. We were given glimpses of how we might better relate to and understand those with whom we were beginning to share a new journey. We became curious as to why God had drawn this particular group of us together and allowed ourselves to wonder, *Why are these characters and stories being drawn together just now? What might God have for us as we continue to allow him to author our individual stories and our shared story?*

As I reflected on why this experience was so compelling, I realized that we had trusted one another with something very precious—our own stories—and in the end, this was the most significant thing we had to offer. We were not sharing a sanitized version of how we wished things were or how we thought things ought to be; what we had to offer was our own true story told with grace and truth, humility and authenticity. Stories, after all, are not meant to be argued with, judged or dismissed; they are meant to be received.

ENCOUNTERING CHRIST IN SCRIPTURE

Helping them find themselves in the story is exactly what Jesus did for the disciples on the Emmaus Road, and it was, indeed, transformative. They had been completely hunkered down in their trauma, and it had been pretty consuming. But there was something bigger going on, and this was the second lens Jesus offered through which to understand the events of the weekend: he was locating their personal experience within the larger story of what God was doing in the world. He drew attention to the fact that the traumatic events that had felt so random and personal up to that point had actually been predicted long ago as part of a much more encompassing plan. *"Beginning with Moses and all the prophets, he interpreted to them the things about himself in all the scriptures."*

Now, rather than seeing themselves as mere victims of forces beyond their control, the disciples became valued participants in His-story—the greatest story ever told. They began to find meaning in the events they had endured rather than dismissing them as senseless acts of violence that left them feeling traumatized and empty. This was more than just a history lesson; they encountered Jesus' transforming presence in and through the biblical story *and* in their own story, and it changed them utterly. Surely this is one aspect of the renewing of our minds that Paul talks about in Romans 12:2—discovering brand-new ways to think about our lives and our stories!

Bonhoeffer describes this practice of finding ourselves in God's story as one element of our "common life under the Word." He points out that when we allow ourselves to be found in the biblical record of God's saving work,

> we become a part of what once took place for our salvation. Forgetting and losing ourselves, we, too, pass through the Red Sea, through the desert, across the Jordan and into the promised land. With Israel we fall into doubt and unbelief and through punishment and repentance experience again God's help and faithfulness. All this is not mere reverie but holy, godly reality. *We are torn out of our own existence and set down in the midst of the holy history of God on earth.* There God dealt with us, and there he still deals with us, our needs and our sins, in judgment and grace. It is not [just] that God is the spectator and sharer of our present life, however important that is; but rather that we are reverent listeners and participants in God's action in the sacred story, the history of the Christ on earth. . . . Only in the Holy Scriptures do we learn to know our own history. The God of Abraham, Isaac and Jacob is the God and Father of Jesus Christ and our Father.[1]

The Role of Scripture in Transforming Community

Engaging Scripture in such a way that we open ourselves to an encounter with the real presence of Christ as we walk together is an essential element of transforming community. Many of us who have been in and around the church for a long time are used to studying Scripture and listening to good preaching and teaching in order to gain information *about* the God who is found in Scripture. Oftentimes we use Scripture as a tool for our own ends—becoming more learned, preparing to lead or participate in a Bible study, teaching and preaching, passing a test or writing a paper (if we are in Bible school or seminary), proving a point (if we're in the midst of an argument with someone).

If we have been shaped by the Protestant tradition, one of our strengths is that by nature we are very Word- and word-centered. The Word of God in Scripture is our highest authority for faith and practice, and the "preached word" is the highest priority in many of our church services. You may have noticed that in many Protestant sanctuaries the pulpit—symbolizing the priority of the Word proclaimed from it—is the centerpiece of the worship space, whereas in traditions such as Catholic, Anglican and Lutheran, the altar is placed centrally as a symbol of the real presence of Christ. This is not to say that either position is right or wrong, better or worse; every tradition has its strengths and its weaknesses, and, in fact, over time our strengths can become our weakness.

In a word-centered tradition, it is possible to be so intent on gaining information *about* the Word that we miss encountering the Word himself. Whereas, in a sacramental tradition, it is possible to experience the more mystical elements of the spiritual life and never engage in a serious study of God's word to us in Scripture. While the study of Scripture is foundational to the Christian life, information alone does not bring about transformation; only a life-changing encounter with Christ can do that. At the same time, the study of Scripture can become a powerful catalyst for life-changing encounters with the Word who became flesh and dwelled among us, full of grace and truth.

When we engage Scripture for spiritual transformation, we are drawn into relationship with Christ, the Living Word. We are engaged not only at the level of the mind but also with our heart, our emotions, our

> In Christianity the Word of God is a person, not a book.
>
> Michael Casey

body, our curiosity, our imagination and our will. We open ourselves to the deeper level of understanding and insight that grows
out of and leads us deeper into a personal relationship with the
One behind the text. We adopt a receptive, listening stance in
which Jesus opens the Scriptures for us in such a way that they
become an instrument of his work rather than a tool we use for our
own ends—no matter how worthy those ends might be. Then, as
we encounter Christ in the text, we respond to what we read with
our whole being—heart, soul, mind and strength. We discover that
transformation is primarily a relational thing, taking place in the
context of a real relationship with a real person—Jesus himself.

TRANSFORMATIONAL READING

When we interact with Scripture as a place of encounter, we pay
attention to our own inner dynamics and allow our responses to
take place in the deeper levels of our being. We open to a whole
different set of questions—questions that help us risk greater
levels of truth telling with ourselves, with God and with the
spiritual companions God has given us. In addition to asking
questions like *What does the text say? What does it mean? How do
I apply it to my life?* (all very cognitive, keeping us in control of
the text), we might also ask:

- How do I feel about what is being said? Where do I find
  myself resonating deeply? Where do I find myself resisting,
  pulling back, disagreeing, wrestling with what the text might
  be saying? Can I be honest with Jesus and with these companions about that?

- Why do I feel this way? What aspect of my life and being is
  being touched, challenged, spoken to through this Scripture?
  What do I want to say to Jesus about that?

- What do my reactions tell me about myself—my attitudes, my relating patterns, my perspectives and behaviors? Can I be with that in God's presence and let him guide me to what is needed?

- As spiritual companions, can we leave the space open and endure the discomfort of being present with each other as we wrestle with what God is saying to each of us in and through the written Word?

What we're talking about here is moving beyond informational reading to transformational reading. Henri Nouwen describes the difference between the two in this way:

> Reading often means gathering information, acquiring new insight and knowledge, and mastering a new field. It can lead us to degrees, diplomas and certificates. Spiritual reading, however, is different. It means not simply reading about spiritual things but also reading about spiritual things in a spiritual way. That requires a willingness not just to read but to be read, not just to master but to be mastered by the words [of Scripture]. As long as we read the Bible or a spiritual book simply to acquire knowledge, our reading does not help us in our spiritual lives. We become very knowledgeable about spiritual matters without becoming truly spiritual people.[2]

The question for transforming communities, then, is, how can we incorporate group practices that help us encounter Christ, the Word made flesh, in and through the pages of Scripture on the road between the now and the not yet? There are three practices that can help.

FINDING YOURSELVES IN THE STORY

A foundational practice for communities that want to engage Scripture for spiritual transformation is the one I described at the beginning of the chapter: finding yourself in the story. Between now and your next gathering, take time to listen and pay attention to the invitation to find yourself in the biblical story and then reconvene to share with one another as described in the opening story. Depending on how large your group is, you may be able to listen through the entire group in one gathering, or you may need to take a couple of meeting times to give everyone ample time to share.

When everyone has had a chance to share their individual stories, you may want to reflect a bit on why God is bringing these particular stories together at this time. How does hearing each one's story offer helpful guidance and sensitivity as you seek to be spiritual companions for one another? What invitation to further transformation is contained in each one's story?

You will never regret the time and attention you give to sharing with one another in this way; it will strengthen you as a community immeasurably.

> ### *For Personal Reflection*
> Ask God to help you discover where you are in the biblical story along the lines described here. Try not to make this an intellectual exercise that you work really hard at. Instead, move through your daily activities prayerfully and attentively with this question in mind, waiting for God to show you.

FOLLOWING THE LECTIONARY

The second practice that keeps us steeped in the flow of Scripture and creates more space for God to be in control is the practice of using a common lectionary. The most widely used these days is the Revised Common Lectionary (1992)—a three-year reading schedule that follows the calendar of the Christian year. Each year is identified simply as Year A, B or C, and each week of each year offers an Old Testament reading, a psalm, an Epistle passage and a Gospel passage that share a common theme.

Following a common lectionary keeps us moving through the seasons of the church year together, ensuring that we engage the full range of Scripture and touch all the major themes of Scripture at least once every three years. Rather than cherry-picking passages from the Scriptures based on what we prefer to read or what we think we need, the use of the lectionary forces us to interact with Scriptures we might otherwise avoid and allows God to surprise us with messages we might otherwise have missed. When we follow a common lectionary we practice surrender, giving ourselves over to Scriptures that have been chosen for us rather than choosing Scripture according to our own agenda. We allow God to bring Scripture to bear on our lives in unexpected ways, as he knows we need them.

Since the lectionary follows the rhythm of the Christian year, we are also surrendering to and being shaped by the life-transforming lessons contained in each season—Advent, Christmas, Epiphany, Lent, Eastertide, ordinary time—and many important days in the life of the church. Each year focuses on one of the Synoptic Gospels (Matthew, Mark and Luke), with John appearing throughout; in this way we immerse ourselves constantly in the life of Christ and allow his life to shape our own.

Most communities that follow the lectionary "read into" the Sunday selections so that when they gather corporately, individuals will hear the Scriptures they have been reading and reflecting on throughout the week. Then on Monday, we start reading the lectionary selections for the upcoming Sunday. This a very unifying and cohesive way of interacting with Scripture in community, even if we are engaged in other Bible studies or preaching series that may be

focused on a chosen theme. To find the lectionary schedule, visit
www.transformingcenter.org/in/transforming-resources/lectionary
-calendar.shtml or lectionary.library.vanderbilt.edu.

One of the best tools our community has found for following
the lectionary together is *A Guide to Prayer* by Rueben Job and
Norman Shawchuck.[3] There are several versions, and in addition
to the Scripture passages themselves, there are prayers and readings
from the Christian classics to accompany each theme.

For Personal Reflection

How do you respond to the idea of using a common lectionary?
If this practice has been a part of your tradition, what impact
has it had on your spiritual life?

PRACTICING *LECTIO DIVINA*

Lectio divina means divine or sacred reading. It is an approach to
reading Scripture that sets us up to encounter the Living Word
speaking to us in and through Scripture in this present moment.
Lectio divina was practiced by the early mothers and fathers of the
Christian faith. Referring to the material being read and also the
method itself, the practice of *lectio divina* is rooted in the belief that
through the presence of the Holy Spirit, the Scriptures are indeed
alive and active as we engage them for spiritual transformation
(Hebrews 4:12). As we make ourselves open and available to God
through this practice, the Scriptures will penetrate to our very
depths.

Lectio is so old that it was originally presented in Latin as a
private discipline utilized by monks and nuns living in religious
communities. It involves a slow, reflective reading of Scripture that

offers us a way of opening to God's initiative rather than being subject to human agendas—our own or someone else's. It involves a delicate balance of silence and word, speaking and listening—the essential rhythm of all effective communication. Periods of silence help us to quiet our inner chaos so that we are prepared to listen and attend to God when he does speak. It also creates space for noticing our own inner dynamics and exploring them in God's presence, which fosters true intimacy.[4]

Lectio divina is experienced in four movements, and learning it is a little like learning how to dance. When we are learning a new dance, we may be somewhat awkward and overly concerned about "getting it right." We watch our feet, trying to get them to do what they are supposed to do. We wonder what to do with our hands. If we are dancing with a partner, we might be clumsy at first as we try to figure out how to move together gracefully. But in the end, the point is to be able to enter into the dance, flow with it, improvise and enjoy the person you are dancing with. It is the same with *lectio divina*. When we are just starting out, we concentrate on following the steps and getting everything in the right order. But eventually as we become more comfortable, the steps become moves in a dance that flows naturally with beauty and pleasure, heart and soul.

What follows is a description of *lectio divina* adapted as a spiritual practice for groups. Although I have chosen English words to describe the process, the Latin words are included in parentheses so that the beauty and the nuance of the original language are not lost. You will want to choose a passage of Scripture no more than six to eight verses in length if it's a story, even less if it's prose. There will be four consecutive readings of the same passage—either by the same person or by four different readers—and with each reading there will be a different question that invites us to engage the passage in a slightly different way. If someone in your group is experienced in *lectio divina*, consider letting him or her lead the first time. Each reading is followed by a brief period of silence, and then there's opportunity to go around the circle and allow each person to share very concisely what they are hearing. Isaiah 43:1-4 is a good passage to start with, or Matthew 14:22-33 or Mark 10:46-52 if you would prefer a story. For your planning, this process will take twenty to thirty minutes, depending on how long the sharing takes in each move.

Begin with a time of **silent preparation (*silencio*)**, which allows group members to become quiet in God's presence and touch their desire to hear from God. Invite members to sit with eyes closed, let the body relax, breathe deeply and become consciously aware of God's presence. Group members can express willingness to hear from God by praying a simple prayer such as "Come Lord Jesus," "Here I am, Lord," or "Speak, Lord, for your servant is listening." You may even want to light a candle to symbolize the presence of the Holy Spirit as your teacher and guide.

Read (*lectio*). In the first movement, the leader reads the passage twice out loud and participants are to "listen for the word or the phrase that strikes you." This might be a word that stands out from all the rest, causes a visceral reaction or brings about a deep sense of resonance or resistance. The mood is gentle, reflective, with a sense of expectancy that God will speak to individuals. After the reading there is brief period (one minute) of silence in which participants remain with the word, savoring it and perhaps repeating the word or the phrase softly to themselves without trying to figure out what it means or why it was given.

When the leader (the designated timekeeper or the person who read) gives the signal that it is time to share, each group member is given the opportunity to say the word or the phrase aloud without comment or elaboration. Participants may say "I pass" if they wish. There is never any forcing or coercion in transforming community— just a real invitation.

Reflect (*meditatio*). The passage is read a second time, and this time participants are invited to reflect on "the way in which my life is touched by this word. What in my life needed to hear this word today?" If the reading is a story, we might ask, "Where am I in this text? What do I experience as I allow myself to be in this story?" The reading is followed by a brief silence in which participants stay present with God with whatever comes. Rather than *thinking too much* about the passage (this is a real discipline), keep coming back to the word or phrase that has been given.

When the leader gives the signal, participants are invited to share their reflections in one or two sentences without elaborating, explaining or justifying their impression. Beginning with phrases like "I hear," "I see" or "I sense" may be helpful. Participants may say "I pass" if they wish.

Respond (*oratio*). As the passage is read a third time, participants are guided to listen for an invitation that might be contained in what they are hearing. Is there an invitation or a challenge for me to respond to? What is my response? This should be one's first, most spontaneous response to what one has heard and may be expressed directly to God in the prayer that comes most naturally. Perhaps Scripture has touched a place of pain, frustration or anger, and we pour out our feelings in the safety of this moment. Perhaps there is a flash of self-knowledge, and we are convicted of some sin. In the silence we feel our remorse and make our confession. Or we might be overwhelmed by some way in which God tells us that he loves us, and in the silence we let tears of love and gratitude flow and just soak in God's love. Perhaps we hear God calling us to something new, and our heart exclaims, *You've got to be kidding!* Whatever our response, we let it find full expression in the moments of silence that follow. (This silence should be a little longer than the others to allow time for a dialogue to take place between each person and God.)

After the silence, the leader gives the signal and each person may share, in a sentence or two, the invitation they are sensing. Again, do not elaborate, explain, justify or comment on what others say. Listen carefully to what the person on your right is saying, as the conclusion of this exercise will be for each person to pray for the person on their right.

Rest (*contemplatio*). The passage is read one last time, and the invitation is for each person to simply rest in God. Like the weaned child in Psalm 131 who has received what it needs from its mother and can now rest with her in peace and quiet, so we rest with God and simply enjoy his presence. Part of what enables us to rest is the assurance that God is the One who will enable us to actually do what he is inviting us to do. In the silence that follows this final reading, each person just rests in what they have heard. "When our response has been played out in all its fury, angst, or exuberance, we come to a place of rest in God. Here there are no expectations, demands, no need to know, no desire but to be in the Divine Presence, receptive to what God desires to do with us."[5]

INCARNATING THE WORD (*INCARNATIO*)

As you emerge from the resting, each person in the group is resolved to incarnate or carry their "word" with them into daily life. As we continue to listen to this word in the context of our ordinary life, we are led deeper and deeper into its meaning as we discover what it means *for us*. In this way the Living Word is being formed in us more fully every day. This adds a new dimension to how you pray for one another as spiritual companions, and you are privileged to witness these incarnations and cheer one another on! It will also provide rich fodder for sharing how each of you is responding to God's invitations in everyday life and what it is like to seek to incarnate the word you have received.

Bonhoeffer encourages and inspires us to

> ponder the chosen text on the strength of the promise that it
> has something utterly personal to say to us for this day and
> for our Christian life, that it is not only God's Word for the
> Church, but also for us individually. We expose ourselves to
> the specific word until it addresses us personally.... We read
> God's Word as God's word for us.... In meditation God's
> Word seeks to enter in and remain with us. It strives to stir
> us, to work and operate in us, so that we shall not get away
> from it the whole day long. Then it will do its work in us,
> without our being conscious of it.[6]

--------- ON THE ROAD TOGETHER ---------

Take time together as a group to discuss the difference between
reading for information and reading for transformation. Allow
each individual to share how they are relating to Scripture personally, and then also discuss how you are using Scripture as a part
of your group life. Is your group's use of Scripture more informational or transformational?

As you reflect on this chapter, what is your desire relative to the
use of Scripture in your group? What are you drawn to? Which
practices would you like to explore and experiment with? Take
time to agree on what you would like to try, and brainstorm ways
of incorporating those practices into your group's life.

You may want to take several meeting times to explore and
practice each method together before deciding exactly how you
will incorporate Scripture in an ongoing way into the life of your
group. First of all, take a meeting or two to give each person a
chance to share where they are finding themselves in the biblical

story and how that knowledge is influencing their lives.

Then explore using a common lectionary for a week or two, and reflect together on what is was like personally and corporately. How did God speak to you personally in surprising ways? What was it like to know that you were all reading the same Scriptures throughout the week? Did it open up any new conversations?

Experiment with *lectio divina*, and do it together. If you are part of a larger community that uses the lectionary, consider using one of the lectionary passages; if not, consider using the passage the pastor preached from the previous Sunday. After you have experienced *lectio* together, reflect on which moves were most meaningful and most challenging. How was it the same as or different from how you usually engage Scripture? What difference has the word you received made in your life?

After you've tried these approaches to Scripture, discuss how you would like to engage Scripture together in an ongoing way.

Help Me Listen

O Holy One,
I hear and say so many words,
Yet yours is the Word I need.
Speak now,
and help me listen;
and, if what I hear is silence,
let it quiet me,
   let it disturb me,
      let it touch my need,
         let it break my pride,
            let it shrink my certainties,
               let it enlarge my wonder.[7]

WERE NOT OUR HEARTS BURNING WITHIN US?

Discerning the Presence of Christ

They urged him strongly, saying, "Stay with us, because it is almost evening and the day is now nearly over." So he went in to stay with them. When he was at the table with them, he took bread, blessed and broke it, and gave it to them. Then their eyes were opened, and they recognized him; and he vanished from their sight. They said to each other, "Were not our hearts burning within us while he was talking to us on the road?"

LUKE 24:29-32

Have you ever had a conversation that felt so good you didn't want it to end? Maybe it was that first date with the person who later became your husband or wife when you kept saying, "What? You too?!" Maybe it happened over coffee with a new friend whom you eventually recognized as a kindred spirit; everywhere you went in conversation, the other person was able to meet you there.

Perhaps it was a small dinner-party group that settled into a deeper and more substantive conversation after the dishes were done and everyone was sipping wine around the fire. Somehow you got to places of openness and honesty that left you feeling there were people who finally "got" you and you weren't so alone after all. Perhaps you risked sharing some heart-holy dream that you rarely talk about and discovered a common vision or a shared passion. People were unusually present with each other, and the few words shared were so thoughtful that a new door or window of insight seemed to just open up. As everyone realized, reluctantly, that it was getting late, you parted ways longing for more of whatever it was that had just taken place.

If you have ever had an experience like that, you know exactly what the disciples on the road to Emmaus felt as they approached the exit to their village and it was time to part ways. The conversation they had been having with Jesus was so *different* in tone, quality and content from what they were used to that they did not want it to end. They longed for more of the freedom to share how they really felt without being judged or fixed. They hungered for the kind of deep listening Jesus was so skilled at—the kind that created space for hard questions and shared silence when emotions ran deep. Even though the conversation with Jesus had been challenging, to say the least, they wanted more of Jesus' paradigm-shifting perspective rather than continuing to settle for mere platitudes. Perhaps the conversation felt strangely familiar even though they couldn't quite pinpoint it.

Even though it was getting dark and it would have been dangerous to be out on the road alone, Jesus pretended to go on—probably because he didn't want to impose on the Middle Eastern manners that would have called for these fellow travelers to offer their new companion a place to stay. But beyond obligatory politeness, "they urged him *strongly* to stay," so Jesus gave in to their friendly persuasion. And that's when things *really* started to get interesting!

THE POWER OF STAYING

The word *stay* is used twice in verse 29 and reminds us that the discipline of staying together is quite significant to the outcome of this story. At the beginning, the two disciples chose to stay with each other and walk together, which opened them to the presence of Christ. Here at the end of the story, *all three* companions choose to stay together, which opened up all sorts of possibilities for further encounter, deeper levels of recognition and true discernment—possibilities that would have been missed if they had left each other too soon.

This aspect of the story is worthy of note because it is so countercultural in our milieu. We live in a global society that is so transient, hardly anyone stays anywhere for very long. People routinely leave family and friends behind in order to follow a job. Couples choose not to stay married when the going gets tough. Congregants leave their churches when they disagree with the pastor or a new, better version of church gets started down the street or across town. Congregations leave denominations when they disagree with policies and practices; denominations splinter and new denominations form when the chasm seems too deep and too wide to be bridged.

One of the reasons Christianity has become irrelevant in our culture is our inability to stay together. Those around us watch all our disagreements, leavings and splittings and see us as no better

off than they are. But this has not always been so. Prior to the
Protestant Reformation, one of the characteristics of faith communities was commitment and stability. In Jewish tradition, there
was literally no place to go for an alternative community of faith—
no smorgasbord of synagogues or denominations to choose from
based on personal preference. One was either part of the local faith
community that worshiped the one true God or on the outside—
spiritually, relationally and economically. Likewise, in the Catholic
tradition, when a family moved into a particular neighborhood it
was understood that they were committing themselves to that
parish for as long as they lived within its borders. To say nothing
of the monastic tradition, in which a person committed herself or
himself to a way of life in a particular religious order and vowed to
remain faithful to that community for life.

The heart of the matter is that stability—committing oneself to
stay faithful to a particular set of relationships—is one aspect of true
discipleship. As Episcopal priest Brian Taylor points out, this is one
way of placing our life in the hands of God, assuming that our transformation is going to take place in the community God has given us.

> The grass is not greener "over there": one must work out one's
> problems with *this* person because if one doesn't, one will
> have to work it out with *that* person. This is precisely what is
> so freeing about the vow of stability . . . to have to work it out
> is to demand growth, as painful as it is, and that is freeing.
> Faithfulness is a limit that forces us to stop running and en-
> counter God, self, and other right now, right here.[1]

Even though your group is probably not a monastic community,
it may be worth considering stability as a transformative discipline.
What might stability look like for your group? What difference
would it make, and what transformative possibilities might it open

up? Such questions might force deeper reflection and conversation about what kind of community would warrant that kind of commitment and how your group could become such a community. And while it might not be appropriate to demand commitment for life, given some of the abuses that are possible, communities gathered for the purpose of spiritual transformation might at least consider stability and staying as a true invitation of the spiritual life. (For a discussion of how we practice stability in the Transforming Center, see appendix B.) Taylor goes on to say,

> It is the failure to commit oneself entirely that blocks creativity in the spiritual life, in the artistic life, in the relational life. Meeting one's obligations with a minimum of commitment may seem like freedom, but it enslaves us to what is fleeting.... Ultimately, the vow of stability is a vow of stability to God. God is the only true eternal rock upon which we can stand. But God calls us into a particular life, to be spent in the company of particular people.... To accept one's life as it is given is to begin to find freedom.[2]

WHEN THE ORDINARY BECOMES EXTRAORDINARY

The choice to stay together was powerful for the three travelers in Luke 24 because it gave them the opportunity to do something very ordinary together—to share a meal—and that meal became the context in which the most significant and revelatory moments of the whole journey took place. In Jewish culture, sharing a meal had special significance because meals were time of solidarity and fellowship—which is why Jesus often got in trouble for who he ate with. At the very least, his choice to stay and share a meal with these disciples was an expression of his desire to renew fellowship with them after all they had been through.

The Emmaus meal was also highly reminiscent of the Last Supper, when Jesus broke bread and shared wine with his disciples for the last time before his crucifixion. Whether these particular disciples were at that final meal or not, they were probably aware of Jesus' statement that he would not eat the Passover meal or drink from the fruit of the vine until the kingdom of God comes (Luke 22:15-18). Whether they realized it or not, this meal was the fulfillment of that statement right there in their midst: the kingdom of God had come in Christ!

If we observe carefully, we might also notice that an odd reversal takes place during this meal. Even though the disciples had invited Jesus into their home as their guest, by the time they sat down for dinner, Jesus was acting more like the host! He was the one who picked up the bread, blessed it, broke it and served it—something the host would typically have done as an act of welcome, hospitality and exercising one's prerogative to be in control of what goes on in one's own home. *How rude!* we might be thinking. *What in the world is going on?*

The shift Jesus made from being the guest to being the host represents a significant turning point on the road between the now and the not yet. It is the shift from the illusion that we are in control of our relationship with Christ and our spiritual journey to an absolute awareness that Jesus is the one guiding, controlling and sustaining our journey. Early in the Emmaus Road experience, Jesus was deferential and took his cues from the disciples. Taking the role of a stranger, he appeared to be tagging along, following their lead, engaging them in conversation at the level they were comfortable with. He let them set the limits, boundaries and pacing of the conversation and went only as far as they were ready and willing to go.

But when he took the bread in his own hand, blessed it, broke it and started passing it around, there was no doubt who was in charge. With this act, he reclaimed his rightful place as their teacher, their Messiah, their risen Lord. As they received the bread from his hand, they were receiving him back into their lives as Lord and Savior. And it was at that precise moment that their eyes were opened and they were finally able to recognize Jesus for who he was. If they had not stayed together, they would have missed the culminating moment of the whole journey!

One of the most consistent themes in the Emmaus story is that in the ordinary moments of our lives, Jesus is simply delighted to show up and join right in. As we become more practiced at recognizing him—on the way home after a long, hard weekend, during an ordinary conversation between friends, in the midst of mourning our losses, as we prepare food and share a meal together—our vision of the present moment is transformed, and we ourselves are deeply changed.

For Personal Reflection

Think back over the last several days, and notice a time when the presence of Jesus made an ordinary moment extraordinary. What was that like for you?

DISCERNMENT IN COMMUNITY

Learning to recognize the presence of Christ in all of life is also called *discernment*. One of my favorite definitions of discernment is from St. Ignatius of Loyola, founder of the Jesuits: "finding God in all things so that we might love and serve God in all." While discernment might sound like a mystical experience that is available only to the gifted few, it

> *The incredible gift of the ordinary!*
> *Glory comes streaming from*
> *the table of daily life.*
> Macrina Wiederkehr

is really much more foundational to the spiritual life than that. Discernment is an increasing capacity to recognize and respond to the presence of Christ—in ordinary moments and also in the larger decisions of our lives. Discernment is a multifaceted thing in Scripture and in Christian tradition.

Discernment, first of all, is a mark of Christian maturity all of us need to cultivate (Romans 12:2; 1 John 4:1). It is also a spiritual gift. This means we can learn about discernment from those who are so gifted (1 Corinthians 12:10), but because it is a mark of spiritual maturity, all of us are called to grow in this essential aspect of the spiritual life.

Discernment is also a habit in which we are invited to notice what gives life and what drains life from us so we can choose life more and more often (Deuteronomy 30:11-20; John 10:10). Scripture refers to "discernment of spirits" or "testing the spirits to see whether they are from God" (1 Corinthians 12:10; 1 John 4:1). This has to do with distinguishing the real from the phony and the true from the false—in the world outside of ourselves and also in the interior world of our own thoughts and motives. As we become more attuned to these subtle spiritual dynamics, we are able to distinguish between what is good (that which is from God and moves us toward God) and what is evil (that which is not from God and draws us away from God).

St. Ignatius is perhaps best known for crafting a set of exercises that helps folks become more discerning, and in these exercises he identifies the inner dynamics *consolation* and *desolation*. Consolation is the interior movement of the heart that gives us a deep sense of life-giving connection with God, others and our most authentic self in God. We might experience it as a sense that all is right with the world, that we are free to be given over to God and to love even in moments of pain and crisis. Consolation is charac-terized by a sense of abundance and life (John 10:10), love (1 John

4:7), freedom in the Spirit (1 Corinthians 3:17) and inner peace regardless of outer circumstances (Philippians 4:7).

Desolation is just the opposite. It is a sense of being cut off from what is good and best—out of touch with God, unable to be given over to love for God and others, not free to be our most authentic self in God, full of inner turmoil. Desolation might also be experienced as being off-center, not being ourselves, full of confusion and maybe even rebellion.

Consolation and desolation are more than mere feelings; they are visceral, in-the-body experiences that are deeper than the "surface chop" of our emotions, and they need not be particularly momentous. In fact, they might seem relatively inconsequential until we learn to pay attention and listen for what they have to tell us. This was exactly what the Emmaus disciples were doing when they reflected back on their day; they were noticing that when Jesus spoke to them, it had a different effect on them from other conversations. They noticed a visceral reaction—their hearts burning within them—when he talked with them on the road. Even the memory of it filled them with deep encouragement as they realized that even when they had felt alone and bereft, Jesus was right there with them! Discernment requires that we be able to notice when our own hearts are burning with the knowledge that Jesus is near; rather than judging or dismissing such experiences, we are curious and wonder what they have to tell us.

Discernment can also be defined as the ability to recognize where God is at work so that we can join God in it. John 9 records another time when a group of disciples were taking an ordinary walk with Jesus and came across a blind man. They asked, "Who sinned, this man or his parents, that he was born blind?" and Jesus' response was to tell them that they were missing the point entirely. The real issue, when we are walking with Jesus, is being able to recognize what God is up to in any given moment so we can join God in it. Jesus responded, "Neither this man nor his parents sinned; he was born blind so that God's works might be revealed in him. We must work the works of him who sent me while it is day" (John 9:2-4). On any given day—no matter where we are or what we are facing—the discernment question is *What is the work of God here in this moment, and how can I join God in it?*

Of course, as well as all of the above, discernment is a spiritual practice we can engage in both personally and corporately when we want to know the will of God regarding a specific decision we are facing. This is what most of us tend to think of when we hear the word *discernment,* but this is only one aspect of it, albeit very significant. Growing in the habit of recognizing the presence of Jesus and what he is up to—in our lives, our community and the world around us—is the best possible preparation for discerning larger decisions when they come along. Surrounding ourselves with at least a few folks who are cultivating discernment and staying with them for the long haul so that we have a history of recognizing Christ together is the surest foundation for discerning the larger decisions that face us.[3]

The context for *all* aspects of discernment is a growing friendship with God cultivated through solitude and silence, prayer and reflection on Scripture, self-knowledge and self-examination, sane rhythms of work and rest, honoring our body's wisdom, spiritual friendship and community. Assisting one another in establishing a way of life that includes these practices *so we can become more discerning* is a primary function of transforming community.[4]

And Then Their Eyes Were Opened

The entire Emmaus Road experience was really an exercise in discerning Christ's presence—on the road, in conversation, in

Scripture, during the meal. The issue never was whether Christ was present in all these moments, for he surely was! The issue was whether the disciples had the capacity to recognize him, and *that* was something that developed by God's grace, over time, as they shared the journey. Their ability to discern the presence of Christ progressed throughout the story: first they saw him as a stranger, then as a traveling companion, then as a teacher, then as a guest, then as a host, and finally as their Messiah and resurrected Lord.

As it turns out, the physical journey from Jerusalem to Emmaus was nothing compared to the journey from "their eyes were kept from recognizing him" (Luke 24:16) to "their eyes were opened, and they recognized him" (24:31). There are real obstacles to discernment, and the truth is, we all have blind spots that prevent us from recognizing the presence of Christ in our lives. One of the primary functions of transforming community is to be a community for discernment in which we assist one another in noticing and eliminating the obstacles to such seeing. A most fruitful line of questioning about what keeps us from recognizing Jesus on our own journey between the now and the not yet emerges directly from the Emmaus Road story.

- Am I so consumed with grief over my losses that I am not able to discern Christ walking alongside me in the pain?

- Have I become so disillusioned by some of my life experiences that I've given up and given in to cynicism?

- Is my vision so myopic—so focused on the details of my life and making everything so relentlessly personal—that I cannot see things from a larger perspective of what God might be up to?

- Is there any way in which I might be like the disciples who were "foolish . . . and slow of heart to believe" (Luke 24:25) all that had been revealed to them?

- Am I so taken with my human wisdom or the wisdom of this world that I cannot recognize the wisdom that comes from God—which often includes the necessary rhythms of suffering and death, burial/waiting and resurrection?

- Am I so focused on myself and my own agenda that I forget to ask, *What is God up to, and how can I join God in it?*

- What else keeps me from discerning Christ's presence?

Spiritual companions can become practiced at gently asking questions that help remove the obstacles from one another's line of vision.

> ### *For Personal Reflection*
> Which of these obstacles most regularly prevents you from recognizing and responding to Christ in your life?

DARK NIGHTS AND BRIGHT MORNINGS

There is no doubt that we have our own obstacles to deal with when it comes to discernment, but according to this story, there are also times when Jesus seems absent because he chooses to be. Right after the disciples' eyes were opened and they recognized him, he promptly disappeared! These sudden disappearances are common in the postresurrection narratives. When Jesus appeared to Mary at the garden tomb, at first she thought he was the gardener; when she finally recognized him, he told her not to touch him and then disappeared. What is that about?

As excruciating as it must have been to lose Jesus again so quickly right when they thought they were getting him back, there was good reason for it. Jesus wanted them to know he was alive, but he also wanted them to learn to relate to him in a new way. Rather than knowing him as an earthly friend and teacher, he wanted them to engage him on a spiritual level. Rather than clinging to past experiences of physical presence, they would need to cultivate faith that goes beyond sight. They were now going to need to recognize and trust that he was always with them, only now his presence was mediated through the Holy Spirit. This would not be easy.

These postresurrection disappearances seem to correspond to the spiritual experience of the dark night of the soul, that time in the spiritual life when a person no longer experiences the nearness of God in the ways that had become familiar. Classic spiritual writers such as John of the Cross and the author of *The Cloud of Unknowing* describe the dark night as God "going behind the cloud." This is not to be cruel but to help us cultivate a more mature faith that is not so dependent on signs and wonders, feelings and experiences. In this dark night we are stripped of our dependency on intellectual and emotional experiences of God, because they are no longer given. We are called upon to exercise pure faith in God in the absence of the kind of "knowing" and "feeling" that characterized earlier parts of our journey; we discover that we cannot force God's hand or make things happen just because we want them to. This is a time of profound letting go and surrender as we give up the last vestiges of our illusion of self-control and self-will along the way to transforming union with God.

It is of utmost importance that spiritual companions learn how to recognize or discern this part of the journey for themselves and each other. That way they can encourage one another to say yes to the deeper journey of faith, rather than trying to "fix" things that cannot and ought not be fixed because God is actually doing a deep work. "As the disciples had to learn not to cling to their past experiences of Jesus, similarly, in the dark night, the Christian needs to open up to a new way of being in God by letting go of false notions and even sweet spiritual experiences. Though the dark night is experienced as a deep emptiness of the senses, it is a blessing because one's faith is being purified."[5]

THE FELLOWSHIP OF THE BURNING HEARTS

Even though Jesus' disappearance must have left the disciples with a deep sense of loss and emptiness, they gained something very important. They now had this experience of their hearts burning within them as Jesus accompanied them on their journey, and they would always be able to recognize it. They were learning how to know Jesus not just by his physical presence but by the impact his presence had on their hearts. Not only that, they had the incredible blessing of spiritual companionship as they were able to speak about their experience openly with each other and affirm that their encounter with Jesus had been real and life-changing.

Now their communion with Jesus on the road and around the table was calling forth a new kind of community that had to do, not so much with grief and loss, but with Christ's presence and activity among them. Their community would never be the same again!

———————— ON THE ROAD TOGETHER ————————

There are several possibilities for your group in response to this chapter.

1. Discuss the practice of stability, what it means for your group and how you might live that out. As a part of that conversation, consider how stability might give more opportunities to share ordinary moments that invite Jesus to draw near as he

did with the disciples. Are there any agreements you would like to make together in this regard?

2. Reflect together on the nature of discernment and the significance of discernment in community. Which facets do you understand well and know how to practice? Which ones would you like more input on? If someone in your group has the gift of discernment, invite them to share how they experience discernment and what they have learned from having that gift. Are there any next steps you would like to take?

3. Have an honest conversation about obstacles to discernment, allowing individuals to share obstacles they are noticing in themselves. Pray for one another that whatever obstacles you are naming will be removed. Use the prayer Paul prays in Ephesians 1:17-18: "I pray that God might give you, [name], a spirit of wisdom and revelation as you come to know him, and that the eyes of your heart may be enlightened as you let go of the obstacles you have just named."

4. Consider the moment when the Emmaus disciples looked back on their day and noticed Jesus' presence and the effect that it had on them. This is a biblical example of the life-transforming practice called the *examen* in Christian tradition. We can also simply call it a Daily Review. Here is how you can practice it together:

   - Take time to quiet yourselves in God's presence.

   - As you continue in silence, simply review the events of your day, starting at the beginning, asking God to show you where he was present with you and you were not aware of it. Move through the different aspects of your day—waking up, showering, eating breakfast, being with your family, working out, getting to work (driving, commuting on a train or a bus, walking, flying), each of the meetings or tasks you engaged in, the people you met and interacted with, decisions you made, your trip home, dinner with family, whatever brings you to the current moment.

- Notice moments of gratitude, love, peace, guidance, authenticity, protection or wisdom that seemed to come from beyond yourself. Notice when you felt that Jesus was near to you in some special way. Those are experiences of consolation. Thank God for them.

- Notice moments of desolation as well—moments that felt empty, confusing, stressful or draining, unworkable or frustrating. Moments when you were not your best self and felt disconnected from God. Notice without judging. If God felt absent, ask him to show you evidence of his presence. If the source of desolation is something you have any control over, ask God what it would look like to choose life next time. If there is an area you know was sinful or in which you fell short of Christlikeness, confess it, receive God's forgiveness and ask for God's help moving forward.

- When the allotted time for silent reflections is up, briefly share moments of consolation, desolation or your hearts burning within you. (To save time, you could break up into groups of two or three for this sharing.) If there is any wisdom or a question that comes as a result of this noticing, share that too. Receive what people share without comment or discussion.

- When everyone has shared, have one person pray and express gratitude to God for guiding you and for the goodness of his ongoing presence.

Over time, you will notice that this practice results in a much greater awareness of God's presence in the ordinary moments of life and fosters a great deal of spiritual intimacy within the group. It also contributes to the group's growth as a community for discernment, which is one of the primary purposes of transforming community.

As you enter into times of discernment and listening, you may want to begin with this prayer followed by a few moments of silence.

Lord,
I believe
    my life is touched by you,
        that you want something for me,
            and of me.

Give me ears
    to hear you,
eyes
    to see the tracing of your finger in all life,
and a heart
    quickened by the motions
        of your Spirit deep within.

Amen.[6]

THEN THEY TOLD WHAT HAD HAPPENED ON THE ROAD

You Are Witnesses of These Things

*That same hour they got up and returned to Jerusalem;
and they found the eleven and their companions gathered
together. They were saying, "The Lord has risen indeed,
and he has appeared to Simon!" Then they told
what had happened on the road, and how
he had been made known to them in
the breaking of the bread.*

LUKE 24:33-35

The story of the disciples' journey on the Emmaus Road doesn't conclude with a nice meal and a good night's sleep, although that would have been a fitting ending to a really big day. These two disciples were so jazzed that sleep was impossible. They had been transformed in Christ's presence—from dazed and dejected wanderers to confident and joyful bearers of good news—and they couldn't wait to tell their story. So *that same hour* they got up and returned to Jerusalem to share their experience with the other disciples and those keeping watch with them. And what they found out was that they were not alone in having experienced the postresurrection Jesus!

There were others who had experienced Jesus' transformed and transforming presence on the other side of that weekend's traumatizing events, and each encounter was unique. Now there was a whole group of Christ-followers who could share stories of how Jesus had made himself known to them. Together they would ponder, celebrate and make meaning out of a journey that had taken them to Jerusalem to experience the birth of a vision and the death of that same vision, had carried them away from the hub of religious activity to a personal encounter with Jesus in the more intimate places of their lives, and then back to Jerusalem, to the very community where it all began.

JOURNEY INWARD, JOURNEY OUTWARD

The journey motif is, of course, the central metaphor in the Emmaus Road account, and it illustrates the key movements in the spiritual life—from the more private and personal encounter with Jesus into the larger community of others who have also encountered Jesus in life-changing ways and then out into the world beyond the community. Jerusalem was the place where all the action was, spiritually speaking. It was the place where the full manifestation of Jesus as the Christ took place and where the community of Jesus was initially formed. And yet it had been necessary for Cleopas and the unnamed disciples to leave the "religious center" in order to encounter Jesus for themselves on the road of their own lives. A little distance was needed in order to create the space in which a more personal, life-changing word from Jesus could be received.

I'm sure that when these two disciples left Jerusalem and returned to Emmaus, it felt like giving up and leaving everything they had hoped for behind, but now they were returning to Jerusalem with the knowledge that Jesus' presence is not restricted to the religious center. Christ-followers can and do encounter Jesus in places that feel lonely and off the beaten path; in fact, sometimes that is exactly what's needed. Sometimes we must withdraw from life as we have come to know it and share an intimate journey with friends in order to fully encounter Jesus. But very shortly—maybe even immediately!—we discover that our transformation is not for ourselves alone. We are drawn back into the larger community of those closest to us—our families, our friends and neighbors, our faith community—to share what we have experienced in Jesus' presence.

As we share stories of transformation with those closest to us and begin working out the implications with each other in community, Jesus appears in our midst continuing to bring his peace, his presence and his perspective (Luke 24:36-37). And it doesn't take long before he commissions us, saying, "You are witnesses of these things." Almost immediately we discover yet another truth of the spiritual life: even as our journey of transformation brings meaning and joy into our own lives, *our transformation in Christ is also for the sake of others who do not yet know him.*

Henri Nouwen points out that chronology is important. The journey inward must precede the journey outward, or else we have no basis for our togetherness with others and nothing to share. The

> The movement flowing from the Eucharist is the movement from communion to community to ministry. Our experience of communion [with Jesus] first sends us to our brothers and sisters to share with them our stories and build with them a body of love. Then, as community, we can move in all directions and reach out to all people.
>
> Henri Nouwen

journey inward eventually leads quite naturally to the journey outward—into community with others who are experiencing the transforming presence of Christ and into some sense of mission in the world beyond. The reason chronology is important is that we must be deeply grounded in the unconditional love of God in order to see and know other people rightly; we must be experiencing transformation in and through the living presence of Christ before we can invite others into the transformational journey. Our transformation at the heart level through real encounters with Christ is then expressed through love for others. This is the rhythm of solitude, community and ministry/mission.[1]

For Personal Reflection

How do you experience the journey inward and the journey outward? Which aspect is more challenging for you—the inner or the outer?

Solitude is the deep inside place where we are with God and God alone—both as a spiritual practice and as an existential reality. Here we experience ourselves as belonging to God and being unconditionally loved by God; we discover our very lives hidden with Christ in God as the bedrock of our identity. Then we emerge from the solitary place to engage in community with others who are experiencing themselves to be the beloved of God, and we discover that through Christ we belong to one another. While we are together, Jesus stands among us and sends us out on a mission to be his witnesses in the world. But evangelism and mission begin with having a story to tell.

EVANGELISM: AN INVITATION TO SPIRITUAL TRANSFORMATION

If the Emmaus Road story tells us anything, it tells us that our own transformation in Christ's presence is what prepares us to have any kind of good news to share with others. In fact, evangelism is *an invitation to spiritual transformation offered by someone who can bear witness to that transformation in their own life.* When this kind of life sharing bubbles up from our own experience, we don't need a pamphlet or a tract or special training; evangelism becomes simply telling what has happened to us on the road and how Jesus has been making the ordinary extraordinary through his presence in our lives. When we share the story of how we have encountered Christ in a transforming way on our own road between the now and the not yet, evangelism becomes so much more than selling an insurance policy regarding life in the hereafter. It becomes an invitation to the kind of deep and lasting change we are all longing for. We are inviting others into the fellowship of the burning hearts, where Jesus' transforming presence starts to make sense out of everything.

As Dallas Willard so eloquently states,

> When the identified people of Christ reach a certain level of growth and don't go on, they limit their evangelistic potential. Why? *Because the witness of the identified people of Christ to the reality of God in their own lives is weak and becomes a testimony to the contrary.* To have earthshaking evangelism, you have to

have a different quality of persons, and that is what spiritual formation is all about.[2]

As it turns out, the best evangelists are people just like the Emmaus Road disciples who can't wait to tell others what happened to them on the road and how Jesus met them.

For Personal Reflection

Do you feel you have a story of transformation to tell?
When was the last time you got to bear witness to the
transforming power of Christ in your own life?

FORMATION, DISCERNMENT AND MISSION

Transformation into the image of Christ is to love the world that Jesus loved and gave his life for. It could not be any other way. As the sacred heart of Jesus is formed in us, we are able to discern loving, God-guided action in the world that Jesus loves. That becomes our mission. We discover that spiritual transformation is both an end in itself (in that a transforming human being brings glory to God) and a means to other ends, in that it enables us to mediate the presence of Christ to the world. We become partakers of the divine nature (1 Peter 1:4) so that Christ is actually present in the world—through us! Being Christ in the world can take many forms:

- evangelism and faith sharing
- giving generously of our resources
- being involved in reconciliation and peacemaking
- working for justice

- engaging the needs of the world with compassion and caring for the poor
- working for the betterment of the human community in Christ's name

All of these are ways we can become Jesus' hands and feet in a world desperate for hope and healing. The important thing is to be able to discern what is ours to do in the midst of it all rather than relying on human wisdom and human strength, which will eventually wear us out. This is why the relationship between spiritual formation and mission is so important. Spiritual formation results in the ability to discern how God is sending us into the world uniquely to do his will. *Mission cannot be discerned without formation, nor can mission be sustained without an ongoing commitment to transformation in Christ's presence.*

As we engage in our mission in the world, we will inevitably experience our human limitations and our need for God's power, God's strength and God's wisdom. We will discover new ways in which we are not like Christ and where we are pushing our agenda (even a good agenda!) in our own strength rather than surrendering to the will of God already at work in the world. We will be driven back to prayer, casting ourselves upon God's mercy for what needs to be done in us and in the world around us. Without an ongoing commitment to spiritual transformation in community, we simply will not make it for the long haul of ministry and mission in the world, because all we will have to bring is our human self, which will never be enough.

Robert Mulholland wisely points out that there will always be "a creative tension between our spiritual pilgrimage and the world in which it is lived out. If we attempt to undo this difficult tension, we move either into an 'unworldly' spirituality that isolates us from the world or into a 'worldly' spirituality that isolates us from the radical demands of a vital relationship with God."[3]

LIVING IN CIRCLES

> Christ has no body now but yours, no hands, no feet on earth but yours. Yours are the eyes through which he looks with compassion on the world, yours are the feet with which he walks to do good. Yours are the hands with which he blesses the world. . . . Christ has no body now on earth but yours.
>
> Teresa of Ávila

It can be helpful to envision the spiritual life as unfolding within concentric circles of relationship. The inside circle is that very private place where we encounter Jesus' transforming presence for ourselves. The next circle out is the community where the journey of transformation is supported and catalyzed in relationship with those closest to us (family, close friends and spiritual companions) and where we experience ourselves to be part of a larger community of a local church, a particular faith tradition and the communion of saints. From community, we move out into the circle of the world to share Christ and minister to others in his name. There we discover our limits and our great need for more of Christ's transforming presence and power, which draws us back to the center again. Moving among all these circles in a balanced way over time is the fundamental rhythm of a deeply spiritual life.

DISCERNING AND DOING THE WILL OF GOD

Spiritual transformation results in an increasing capacity to *discern* the will of God so we can actually *do* God's will in the world. This is how spiritual formation and mission come together in fruitful synergy for the good of all. As we draw close to Christ, who had the courage and will to lay down his life for the sake of others according to God's purposes, we too find the courage to do what God asks us to do on behalf of the world he longs to save. And the whole process takes place in transforming community, where we assist one another in discerning what God is calling us to do and support one another in saying yes to God's risky invitations.

We might even discover that there is a *shared* mission God has in mind for us as well—something we are called to do together for the sake of the world. Then together we will learn how to live within a constellation of beautiful paradoxes that are held together in creative tension. Love for God and love for neighbor. Solitude and community. Silence and word/Word. Prayer and action. Work and rest. Discerning and doing the will of God. Formation and mission. Just like the disciples who journeyed from Jerusalem to Emmaus and back again, we will learn how to move into the center and out and then back again; and at every point along the way, Jesus' presence is there, causing our hearts to burn within us as we walk the road together.

——————— ON THE ROAD TOGETHER ———————

Take time to look back on your own walk to Emmaus, and notice how your journey of transformation has carried you deeper into the world for the sake of others or has caused you to be in the world *differently* for the sake others.

Then consider how God has used your engagement with the world in Christ's name to foster and even catalyze deeper levels of transformation in you. Affirm this in one another and celebrate it together.

As you reflect on your experience of transformation together, are you sensing God calling you to reach beyond yourselves to touch a wider world? Is there a mission emerging among you—something your little band of Christ-followers is being called to be or to do in Jesus' name?

A PRAYER FOR GOING FORTH INTO THE WORLD

(Leader reads lowercase and everyone reads uppercase together.)

Let us stand and pray together:

As Abraham left his home and the security of all he had
known,

SO WE LAY DOWN WHAT IS PAST AND LOOK TO THE FUTURE.

As Mary washed Jesus' feet with oil and hair,

SO WE TAKE INTO DAILY LIFE SIGNS OF HOPE AND HEALING.

As the disciples returned to Jerusalem to tell what had
happened on the road,

as John built community and Paul traveled ever on,

SO WE REACH BEYOND OURSELVES

TO SHARE THE LIVES OF OTHERS AND TOUCH A WIDER
WORLD.

As Esther stepped out in faith for such a time as this,

SO WE TAKE COURAGE TO DO WHAT GOD CALLS US TO DO.

And as Jesus taught us, so we say:

OUR FATHER IN HEAVEN, HALLOWED BE YOUR NAME.

YOUR KINGDOM COME, YOUR WILL BE DONE ON EARTH AS IN
HEAVEN.

GIVE US TODAY OUR DAILY BREAD.

FORGIVE US OUR SINS AS WE FORGIVE THOSE WHO SIN
AGAINST US.

LEAD US NOT INTO TEMPTATION, BUT DELIVER US FROM EVIL.

FOR THE KINGDOM, THE POWER AND THE GLORY ARE YOURS,

NOW AND FOREVER. AMEN.[4]

GRATITUDES

We speak of what we know and testify to what we have seen.

JOHN 3:11

As the writing of this book comes to a close, I am full of gratitude for the communities I have been privileged to be a part of and keenly aware of how each one has contributed to the shaping of this work.

First of all, I am grateful to the communities of the Transforming Center, without whom this book might never have been written. Fifteen years ago, when our two-year Transforming Community experience first started to emerge, we needed a fresh, biblical approach to community, and God drew me into the Emmaus Road narrative as a model for what we were trying to be and to do. I will never forget what it was like to receive that message for myself first and then offer it to all of us who were embarking on the journey of transforming community together. Thanks to all who have responded so deeply, allowing this story to continually inspire us to walk together on the journey between the now and the not yet, against all odds.

Special thanks to Dalene, whose commitment to walking with me and holding my vocational life together grounds me in the experience of transforming community every day; to her husband, David, for always being there for both us; and to the board, staff and volunteers of the Transforming Center for the privilege of ministering in community. It would not be possible to write a book like this without a community to live it with; the stability of our relationships over the years is continual affirmation that transforming community really is possible.

I am grateful for the companionship of spiritual friends—Brenda, Adele and Marilyn—and for my brothers, Jonathan Taylor Haley and Bill Haley, whose presence on the journey continually enriches my life and calls out the best in me.

I am ever thankful for my friends and colleagues at InterVarsity Press—Bob, Cindy, Jeff and all the team members who support the process—for such a fruitful publishing partnership.

And of course, my deepest gratitude goes to the transforming community that is my family: to my husband, Chris, whose support is unfailing. To our beautiful daughters and their loving husbands—Charity and Kyle, Bethany and Ryan, Haley and Troy—who are my favorite people in all the world. To our grandchildren—Gabriel, Thomas, Finley, Hannah, Joseph and one on the way—who bring more joy to my life than I could ever have imagined. And to my parents, Charles and JoAnn, who pray for me continually. Joan Chittister points out that "the family is not just a routine relationship; it is our sanctification," and that is my experience every day. Our life together in Christ produces the sweetest fruit!

Appendix A

BIBLICAL PERSPECTIVES ON SPIRITUAL TRANSFORMATION IN COMMUNITY

I am ... in labor until Christ is formed in you.

GALATIANS 4:19 (NASB)

The fact that we as human beings can be transformed into the image of Christ is one of the great promises of the gospel and is central to life in the Christian community. If you are interested in taking a closer look at some of the biblical themes referred to throughout this book, following are some Scripture passages you may want to reflect on grouped by topic.

A definition. Spiritual transformation is the process by which Christ is formed in us for the glory of God, for the abundance of our own lives, and for the sake of others (Galatians 4:19; Romans 8:29; 2 Corinthians 3:18; Romans 12:1-2; Colossians 1:28-29).

Renewing the mind. Spiritual transformation takes place

through the renewing of the mind (Romans 12:2), whereby we are actually able to "let the same mind be in you that was in Christ Jesus" (Philippians 2:5-13; Ephesians 4:17-24).

The mysterious work of the Holy Spirit. Spiritual transformation is something only God can accomplish in our lives through the work of the Holy Spirit, who is our advocate, teacher and counselor (John 3:8; John 15 and 16; 1 Corinthians 2:9-16; Galatians 5:22-25).

Paul alludes to the paradox of the natural and the supernatural in the spiritual life by using two metaphors—the formation of an embryo in its mother's womb (Galatians 4:19) and metamorphosis, referring to the process by which a caterpillar enters into the darkness of the cocoon in order to emerge, eventually, changed almost beyond recognition (Romans 12:2). Both are natural phenomena in the physical world, but there is also something about each that is purely a God thing. Both metaphors indicate an element of mystery—that is, something that is outside the range of normal human activity and that can only be understood through divine revelation and brought about by divine activity. Everything we affirm as central to our Christian faith—including transformation—is somewhere in Scripture referred to as a mystery:

- the mystery of God (1 Corinthians 2:1)

- we are servants and stewards of God's mysteries (1 Corinthians 4:1)

- the mystery of God's will (Ephesians 1:9)

- the mystery of Christ (Ephesians 3:4)

- the mystery of the gospel (Ephesians 6:19)

- the mystery of marriage applied to Christ and the church (Ephesians 5:31-32)

- the mystery of Christ in you, the hope of glory (Colossians 1:27)

- God's mystery, which is Christ himself (Colossians 2:2)
- the mystery of the faith (1 Timothy 3:9)

The role of spiritual disciplines (Romans 12:2).

Spiritual disciplines are the main way we offer our bodies up to God as a living sacrifice. We are doing what we can do with our bodies, our minds, our hearts. God then takes this simple offering of ourselves and does with it what we cannot do, producing within us deeply ingrained habits of love and peace and joy in the Holy Spirit.[1]

The role of community in spiritual formation (Romans 12; 1 Corinthians 12; Ephesians 4). We change incrementally over time in relationships with others as we find ways to open to God together.

For the sake of others. Mature spirituality is measured by an increasing of our capacity to love God and to love others (Mark 12:30-31; 1 Corinthians 13; 1 John 4:7). Spiritual formation is both an end in itself, in that it brings glory to God, and a means to discern God-guided action in the world (Isaiah 58:6-14; Micah 6:8; Matthew 28:18-20; Mark 12:30-31).

For a more complete interactive guide to these Scriptures, see Ruth Haley Barton, *Spiritual Transformation: A Biblical & Theological Perspective* (Wheaton, IL: Transforming Resources, 2013), available at ttcbooks.myshopify.com/products/spiritual-transformation-a-biblical-theological-perspective. (Suitable for use as a group Bible study or for personal use.)

Appendix B

PRACTICING STABILITY

*We bind ourselves to each other in times of strength so
that in moments of weakness we do not become unbound.*

JEFF GREENWAY

One of the ways we practice stability in the Transforming Center is
to make a covenant with each other which addresses many aspects
of community life—including stability. Participants in our two-year
Transforming Community® experience sign a covenant when they
begin (see below), and those who are part of the Transforming
Center in a long-term way sign and renew a covenant annually. We
do this because we are convinced that the richest fruits of community life do not grow in a garden of uncertainty, and we assume
that these are the people God has given us to grow with, even when
the going gets tough. We understand that if we don't work our stuff
out here in this community, we will probably meet the same issues
(and ourselves!) in the next community we attach ourselves to.

With great respect for the fact that change happens and it is

God's prerogative to lead his people on in his time and in his way, we also know there are unique spiritual benefits that come to us in the context of long-term commitment. Consequently, one of our most significant covenant commitments is that we will not leave each other unless and until we discern it together. This means we do not have to live in fear and uncertainty that at any moment someone might pick up and leave without processing it with anyone. And it means we can continue to deepen our relationships and commitment to each other, knowing that if the winds of God-guided change do begin to blow, we will have the opportunity to work through a process together so we can affirm a shared sense of God's leading.

Journeying together as a spiritual community is a commitment to nurture one another's desire for God and to support one another in seeking a way of life that is consistent with that desire. Following is an adapted version of the covenant we sign at the beginning our of our two-year Transforming Community experience.

I/we commit to these practices:

- Stay together until the end of the two-year process unless *together* we discern otherwise.

- Communicate ahead of time when I will need to be late or miss a meeting so the group knows to not expect me and so I can stay connected on the journey.

- Be faithful to my own personal rhythm of spiritual practices so that I am bringing a transforming self to this community.

- Pay attention to those times when "our hearts burned within us" and "Christ was made known to us on the way." Be willing to share this as appropriate.

- Cultivate self-awareness and be self-disclosing as appropriate.

- Respect each other's personal relationship with God, recognizing that each one's relationship with God takes place at *God's initiative* and is God's to control.

- Create a safe place for being with strong emotion and unresolved questions. (Listen rather than fix. Ask questions rather than give easy answers.)
- Support and pray for one another as we seek to cultivate a rhythm of spiritual practices that creates space for God's activity in our lives.
- Respect and value diversity.
- Speak the truth with love and grace. Be committed to speak with each other and with presenters when misunderstanding or offense takes place, in order to prevent any hindrance to full participation and growth.
- Practice conflict transformation along the lines of Matthew 5:23-24 and Matthew 18:15-20.
- Honor confidentiality. What is shared in the group will be held in confidence among those who were present when it was shared.
- Honor community by refusing to keep secrets from one another that affect the life of the group.
- Respect intellectual property. [This one probably will not be applicable to most groups.]
- Unplug from technology when we are together.
- Consider emails from the group to be important communication regarding our journey together and respond in a timely fashion. Be committed to not clogging group members' inboxes with extraneous and unnecessary emails.
- Practice financial faithfulness. In a church community, this might apply to tithing. In a small group, this might be a commitment to sharing hospitality and related expenses equitably.
- **Call each other back to these commitments whenever it feels like we're slipping or the covenant has been broken.**

Before ratifying this covenant, we give ample time to discuss the following questions: Is there anything else that is important to you that will help you "lean into" the experience of spiritual community? Is there any part of this covenant where you feel hesitancy, fear or resistance? Do you feel ready to covenant with this community regarding these commitments?

The covenant can be ratified (made real) through a symbolic action such as signing a written document, placing a stone on the altar, sharing communion or anything else that has meaning for the group. The following prayer might also be used.

Prayer of Intention

O God, you have taught us to keep all your commandments
by loving you and our neighbor:
Grant us the grace of your Holy Spirit, that we may be
devoted to you
with our whole heart,
and united to one another with pure affection;
through Jesus Christ our Lord, who lives and reigns with you
and the Holy Spirit,
one God, for ever and ever. Amen.[1]

NOTES

INTRODUCTION

[1]In his writings, Robert Mulholland repeatedly uses the phrase "agents of God's grace" to describe our relationship with one another in the body of Christ. See *Invitation to a Journey* (Downers Grove, IL: InterVarsity Press, 1993), p. 142. I have also heard him use "agents of God's troubling grace" in his teaching.

[2]Mulholland, *Invitation to a Journey*, p. 145.

CHAPTER 1: BETWEEN THE NOW AND THE NOT YET

[1]Dietrich Bonhoeffer, *Life Together* (New York: Harper & Row, 1954), pp. 26-27.

[2]Ibid., pp. 28-29.

[3]Richard Rohr, *Everything Belongs* (New York: Crossroad, 1999), p. 132.

[4]This is the briefest possible summary of Keating's teaching on this subject. For more, see Thomas Keating, *The Human Condition* (New York: Paulist, 1999).

CHAPTER 2: AND JESUS HIMSELF CAME NEAR

[1]Henri Nouwen, *With Burning Hearts* (Maryknoll, NY: Orbis Books, 1994), pp. 68-69.

[2]St. Benedict, *Saint Benedict's Rule: A New Translation for Today*, trans. Patrick Barry (Herefordshire, UK: Ampleforth Abbey, 1997), pp. 63-64.

[3]*Iona Abbey Worship Book* (Glasgow, UK: Wild Goose, 2001), p. 64.

CHAPTER 3: THEY STOOD STILL LOOKING SAD

[1]Dietrich Bonhoeffer, *Life Together* (New York: Harper, 1954), p. 97.

[2]Ibid., pp. 97-98.

[3]Parker Palmer, *A Hidden Wholeness* (San Francisco: Jossey-Bass, 2004), pp. 61-62.

[4]Mary Sharon Moore, "Listening the Other into Free Speech," *Presence*, March 2008, pp. 29-33.

[5]This list is loosely adapted from Mary Sharon Moore's article (ibid.), with some additions of my own.

[6]From Shalem Institute brochure, Group Spiritual Direction training program, 1993.

[7]I highly recommend Rose Mary Dougherty, *Group Spiritual Direction* (New York: Paulist, 1995); Tilden Edwards, *Spiritual Director, Spiritual Companion* (New York: Paulist, 2001); and Alice Fryling, *Seeking God Together* (Downers Grove, IL: InterVarsity Press, 2008).

[8]Adapted from Contemporary Collect 23: For Education, in *The Book of Common Prayer* (New York: Church Publishing, 1979), p. 261.

CHAPTER 4: BUT WE HAD HOPED . . .

[1]Thomas Merton, *My Argument with the Gestapo* (New York: Doubleday, 1969), pp. 160-61.

[2]Phillip Sheldrake, *Befriending Our Desires* (Notre Dame, IN: Ave Maria, 1994), p. 21.

[3]Rose Mary Dougherty, *Group Spiritual Direction: Community for Discernment* (New York: Paulist, 1995), p. 37.

[4]Ronald Rolheiser, *The Holy Lodging* (New York: Doubleday, 1999), p. 5.

[5]Dougherty, *Group Spiritual Direction*, p. 14.

CHAPTER 5: SOME WOMEN OF OUR GROUP ASTOUNDED US

[1]While some theologians have interpreted this passage to mean that woman was somehow subordinate because she was created to be man's helper, elsewhere in Scripture the same Hebrew word (*ezer*) is most often used in reference to God himself. For example, in Exodus 18:4, Jethro names his son Eliezer because "the God of my father was my help [*ezer*]." And in Psalm 40:17, as in many other places, the psalmist refers to God as "my help [*ezer*] and my deliverer." The word *ezer* is translated in other places in Scripture as "succorer," "rescuer," "deliverer," "strength" and "power." In biblical usage, the word *helper* most often connotes strength—the one who helps is the one who has *something to offer* the one who is helpless or needs help. Adam needed help. He had no partner, so God provided a partner with no hint of either superiority or subordination.

[2]For a more complete treatment of themes related to men and women in community, see Ruth Haley Barton, *Equal to the Task: Men and Women in Partnership at Work, at Church, at Home* (Downers Grove, IL: InterVarsity Press, 1998); Mary Stewart Van Leeuwen, *Gender and Grace* (Downers Grove, IL: InterVarsity Press, 1990); and Ronald W. Pierce and Rebecca Merrill Groothuis, eds., *Discovering Biblical Equality* (Downers Grove, IL: InterVarsity Press, 2005).

[3]Celia Allison Hahn, *Sexual Paradox: Creative Tensions in Our Lives and Congregations* (Cleveland, OH: Pilgrim, 1991), p. 11.

[4]Adapted from *Iona Abbey Worship Book* (Glasgow: Wild Goose, 2001), pp. 16-18.

CHAPTER 6: WAS IT NOT NECESSARY THAT THE MESSIAH SHOULD SUFFER?

[1]David Benner, *The Gift of Being Yourself* (Downers Grove, IL: InterVarsity Press, 2004), p. 90.

[2]Ibid.

[3]Thomas Keating, *The Human Condition* (New York: Paulist, 1999), p. 38.

[4]Richard Rohr, *Richard's Daily Meditations,* November 14, 2009, adapted from *Near Occasions of Grace* (Maryknoll, NY: Orbis Books, 1993).

CHAPTER 7: HE EXPLAINED THE SCRIPTURES TO THEM

[1]Dietrich Bonhoeffer, *Life Together* (New York: Harper, 1954), pp. 53-54, italics mine.

[2]Henri Nouwen, *Bread for the Journey* (New York: HarperOne, 1997), entry for April 15.

[3]Communities can choose from several different versions, all from Upper Room Books: *A Guide to Prayer for All God's People* (1990), *A Guide to Prayer for Ministers and Other Servants* (1980), *A Guide to Prayer for All Who Walk with God* (2013).

[4]Although Bible study is not a part of the *lectio* process itself, Bible study is an essential supplement to it. *Lectio* can actually be used as a powerful follow-up to more traditional Bible study methods, moving people very naturally into the process of application. An excellent resource helping us experience the interplay between Bible study and *lectio divina* is *Contemplative Bible Reading* by Richard Peace (Colorado Springs: NavPress, 1998).

[5]Marjorie Thompson, *Soulfeast* (Nashville: Upper Room Books, 1995), p. 24.

[6]Bonhoeffer, *Life Together,* p. 82.

[7]Ted Loder, *Guerrillas of Grace* (Minneapolis: Augsburg, 1981), p. 31.

CHAPTER 8: WERE NOT OUR HEARTS BURNING WITHIN US?

[1]Brian Taylor, *Spirituality for Everyday Living* (Collegeville, MN: Liturgical, 1989), p. 17.

[2]Ibid., p. 19.

[3]For more on personal discernment, see Ruth Haley Barton, *Sacred Rhythms: Arranging Our Lives for Spiritual Transformation* (Downers Grove, IL: InterVarsity Press, 2006), chap. 7. For more on discernment in community, see Ruth Haley Barton, *Pursuing God's Will Together: A Discernment Practice for*

Leadership Groups (Downers Grove, IL: InterVarsity Press, 2012).

[4]For more complete guidance on the spiritual disciplines mentioned here, see Barton, *Sacred Rhythms*. In fact, this may be a good next step for your group; a group guide is included.

[5]Ekman P. Tam, "The Road to Emmaus: A Biblical Rationale for Sprritual Direction," *Presence*, June 2008, p. 63.

[6]Adapted from Ted Loder, *Guerrillas of Grace* (Minneapolis: Fortress Press, 2005), p. 29.

CHAPTER 9: THEN THEY TOLD WHAT HAD HAPPENED ON THE ROAD

[1]From a recording by Henri Nouwen titled "Solitude, Community and Ministry."

[2]Dallas Willard, in response to a question about the connection between spiritual formation and evangelism, at a staff day at Willow Creek Community Church, April 1999.

[3]Robert Mulholland, *Invitation to a Journey: A Roadmap for Spiritual Formation* (Downers Grove, IL: InterVarsity Press, 1993), p. 161.

[4]Adapted from *Iona Abbey Worship Book* (Glasgow, UK: Wild Goose, 2011), pp. 24-25.

APPENDIX A

[1]Richard Foster, *Renovaré Perspective,* April 1999.

APPENDIX B

[1]From *The Book of Common Prayer*.

formatio

TRADITION. EXPERIENCE.
TRANSFORMATION.

Formatio books from InterVarsity Press follow the rich tradition of the church in the journey of spiritual formation. These books are not merely about being informed, but about being transformed by Christ and conformed to his image. Formatio stands in InterVarsity Press's evangelical publishing tradition by integrating God's Word with spiritual practice and by prompting readers to move from inward change to outward witness. InterVarsity Press uses the chambered nautilus for Formatio, a symbol of spiritual formation because of its continual spiral journey outward as it moves from its center. We believe that each of us is made with a deep desire to be in God's presence. Formatio books help us to fulfill our deepest desires and to become our true selves in light of God's grace.

TRANSF⊕RMING CENTER®
Strengthening the Soul of Your Leadership

The best thing you bring to leadership is your own transforming self!

The Transforming Center exists to strengthen the souls of pastors, Christian leaders, and the congregations and organizations they serve. Don't just learn about spiritual transformation —experience it in your own life!

Ruth Haley Barton (doctor of divinity, Northern Seminary) is founder of the Transforming Center.

Visit the Transforming Center online to learn more about:

- Transforming Community®, a two-year experience of spiritual formation for leaders

- Earning a doctor of ministry, a master's specialization or a certificate in spiritual transformation

- Regional and national pastors' retreats

- Onsite teaching and spiritual guidance for your staff and elders

- Teaching and transformational experiences for your congregation

- *Transforming Church*® initiative

- *Transforming Resources*®—print and electronic

Join thousands of pastors and Christian leaders . . .
subscribe today to our free *eReflections*, spiritual guidance via email.

To subscribe, visit:
www.TransformingCenter.org

TRANSFORMING RESOURCES®
A Ministry of the Transforming Center®

Tools to guide leaders and their communities
in experiencing spiritual transformation.

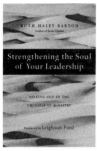

*Strengthening the Soul
of Your Leadership*

Longing for More

*Pursuing God's
Will Together*

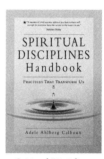

*Spiritual Disciplines
Handbook*

Sacred Rhythms

Sacred Rhythms DVD
curriculum

*Invitation to Solitude
and Silence*

Life Together in Christ

Invitations from God

To see the complete library of Transforming Resources, visit:
www.Resources.TransformingCenter.org

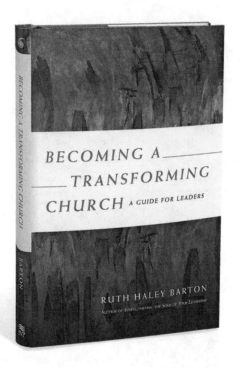

AVAILABLE FALL 2016